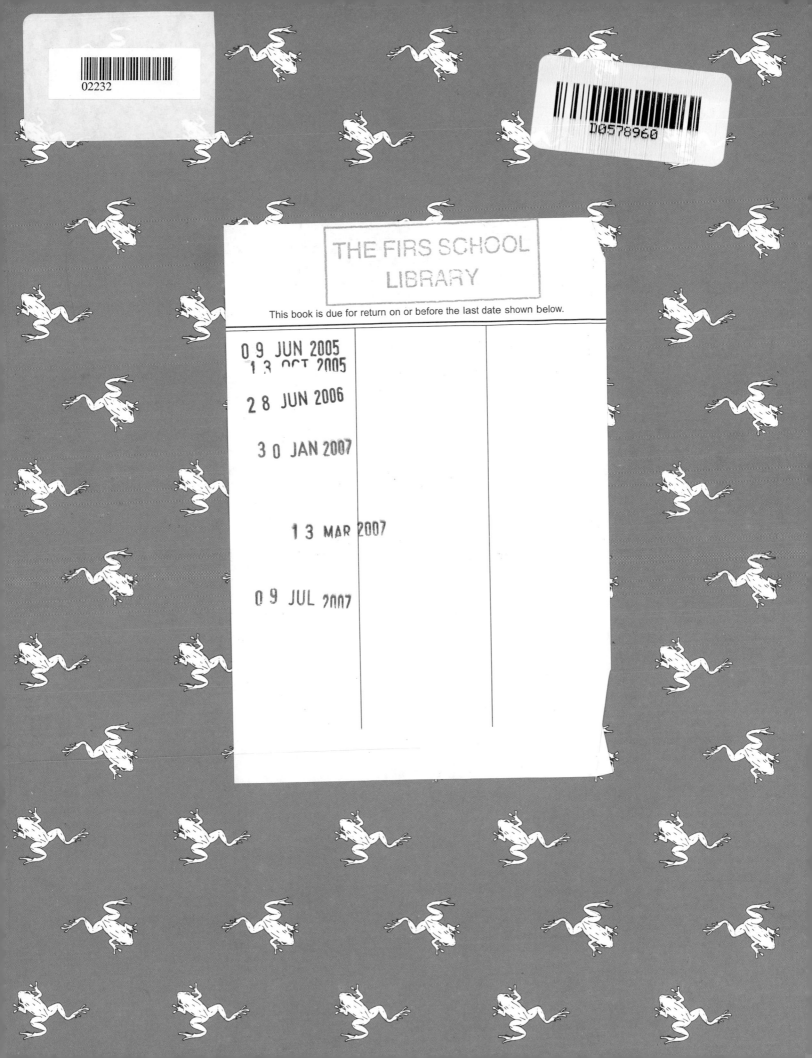

EYEWITNESS ◉ GUIDES

POND
& RIVER

Swan mussel shell

Common reed

Common reed fruiting head

Water snail shell

Otter skull

Kingfisher skull

Mayfly

Reedmace fruit

Reed bunting nest and eggs

Mallard egg

Great diving beetle

Kingfisher wing

Bittern egg

Snipe egg

Banded demoiselle damselfly

Great ramshorn shell

EYEWITNESS  GUIDES

POND & RIVER

Written by
STEVE PARKER

Wandering snail shells

Great pond snail shell

Trout

Hornwort

Tufted duck skull

Teasel heads

Southern hawker dragonfly

Pintail feather

DK

DORLING KINDERSLEY • LONDON
in association with
THE NATURAL HISTORY MUSEUM • LONDON

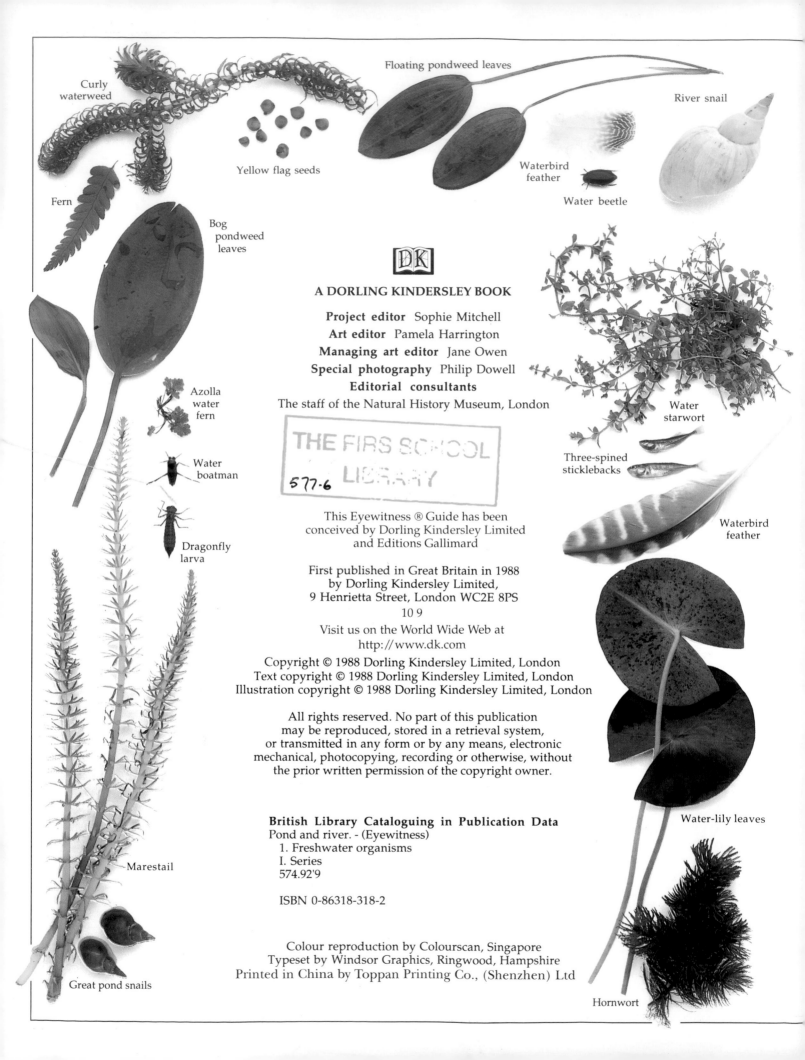

Curly waterweed

Floating pondweed leaves

River snail

Yellow flag seeds

Fern

Waterbird feather

Water beetle

Bog pondweed leaves

Azolla water fern

Water boatman

Dragonfly larva

Marestail

Great pond snails

Water starwort

Three-spined sticklebacks

Waterbird feather

Water-lily leaves

Hornwort

DK

A DORLING KINDERSLEY BOOK

Project editor Sophie Mitchell
Art editor Pamela Harrington
Managing art editor Jane Owen
Special photography Philip Dowell
Editorial consultants
The staff of the Natural History Museum, London

This Eyewitness ® Guide has been
conceived by Dorling Kindersley Limited
and Editions Gallimard

First published in Great Britain in 1988
by Dorling Kindersley Limited,
9 Henrietta Street, London WC2E 8PS
10 9
Visit us on the World Wide Web at
http://www.dk.com

British Library Cataloguing in Publication Data
Pond and river. - (Eyewitness)
1. Freshwater organisms
I. Series
574.92'9

ISBN 0-86318-318-2

Colour reproduction by Colourscan, Singapore
Typeset by Windsor Graphics, Ringwood, Hampshire
Printed in China by Toppan Printing Co., (Shenzhen) Ltd

Contents

Great ramshorn shell

Fool's watercress leaf

Hornwort leaf

6
Spring plants
8
Spring animals
10
Early summer plants
12
Early summer animals
14
Midsummer plants
16
Midsummer animals
18
The pond in autumn
20
The pond in winter
22
Freshwater fish
26
The trout
28
Waterfowl
30
Waterbirds
32
Rushes and reeds
34
The reed bed
36
Waterside mammals
38
Frogs, toads and newts

40
Hunters in the water
42
Floating flowers
44
Plants at the pond's surface
46
Underwater weeds
48
Dragonflies and damselflies
50
Insects in the water
52
Freshwater shells
54
Head of the river
56
Life along the riverbank
58
The river's mouth
60
The saltmarsh
62
Study and conservation
64
Index

Spring plants

AFTER THE DULL, COLD DAYS of winter, spring is here at last. The days are lengthening and temperatures are rising. For plants, it is the beginning of the annual race for a place in the sun. In general the tiny algae, duckweeds and other small plants are first to show their growth, since each individual plant is small and needs relatively few nutrients to increase in size. But around the pond, and in marshy areas elsewhere, the irises, reeds and other colonizers are also showing new, green shoots and leaves. All the plants shown below were collected from around a pond on a spring day - they give an idea of the species you may find, although there will always be variations from pond to pond.

👉 **WARNING**
All the plants and animals shown in this book were collected only after gaining permission from the relevant organisations. Always observe the wildlife and country codes when collecting specimens. 👉

Water crowfoot is one of the first pond flowers to appear in spring

Mature male flowerhead

Great pond sedge

REEDS REBORN
New shoots of reed grass spring up from a tangle of rooting stems and roots, in the marshy area adjacent to the pond or river. One of last year's stems still stands erect, tall as a person.

Immature female flowerhead

Last year's stem persists through the winter

Common sedge

Reed grass

POLLEN AT ITS TIP
This great pond sedge already has one of the male flowerheads at its tip with stamens open and shedding yellow pollen. The female flowerheads are carried lower on the stem; these are not yet mature.

SEDGE AT THE EDGE
Beside the pond grows common sedge, its flowerheads not quite fully opened as yet.

SPRING LILAC
Some of the earliest splashes of colour around the pond are the pale lilac blooms of the cuckoo flower, or lady's smock.

New spring growth

Lady's smock

SEASON OF CATKINS
Willows, common trees of lake and river edges, greet spring with a fine display of furry catkins. These are the tree's flowers. Early bees and other insects visit the flowers for nectar and pollen, and act as pollinators. The wind also blows pollen from the golden male catkins to the greenish female ones, which are usually borne on a different tree.

Female catkins

Goat (pussy) willow

Weeping willow

Female catkins

Crack willow

FLAGS STILL FURLED
The yellow flag iris will soon be in bloom. Here, the new leaves grow up from the thick, spreading, underground stem. Their sword-like shape has given this plant the alternative name of sword flag.

Yellow flag

Sword-like leaves

THE PUSS MOTH
The caterpillar of this moth feeds on sallow, a kind of willow, and poplar leaves. Both these trees are common in damp or moist soils, so puss moths and their caterpillars are often seen near ponds and rivers.

Male catkins covered in yellow pollen

Last year's stem

KING OF THE FLOWERS
The brilliant yellow flowers of the marsh marigold, or kingcup, decorate pond edges and other damp areas almost as soon as the snows melt away. A snail or some other herbivore has already made a meal of one new leaf.

WATER PLANTAIN
A pale, woody stem is all that is left of last year's metre-high (3-ft) spray of flowers (p. 57). New leaves grow from a bulb-like base. Despite its name, the water plantain is not one of the true plantains, bane of the keen lawn gardener.

New spring growth

Marsh marigold

Leaf damaged by snail

Meadow rue

Delicate, notched leaves

Water plantain

SPRING FLUSH
A young meadow rue bears its first flush of distinctively notched leaves. It prefers damp meadows and pond or stream banks.

Spring animals

As the spring sun's warmth spreads through the water, animals begin to stir themselves from among the weeds and mud at the bottom of the pond. It is a time of urgent new life. Frogs and toads, fish and newts, are courting, mating and laying eggs. Their offspring soon hatch in the warming water, eager to cash in on the spring burst of life that provides food for all. "Cold-blooded" aquatic creatures become more active with the rising water temperature, and in a mild spring the smaller ponds, which warm up faster than large ones, are soon seething with newborn snails, insects, amphibians and many other creatures.

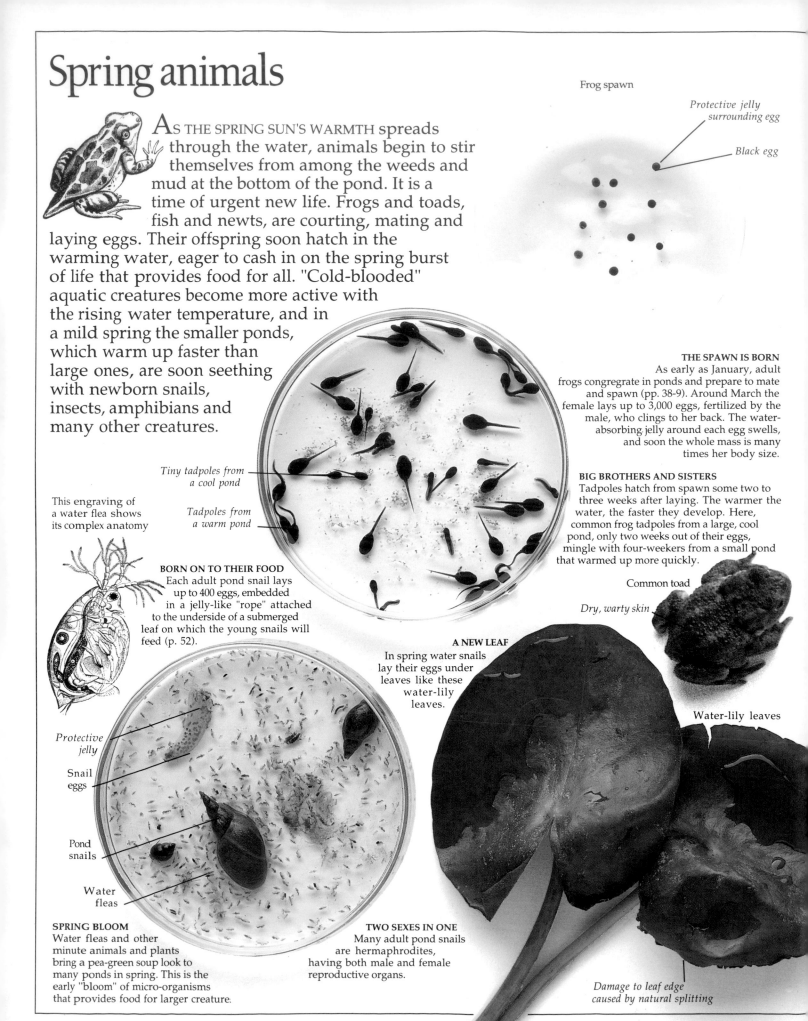

Frog spawn

Protective jelly surrounding egg

Black egg

Tiny tadpoles from a cool pond

Tadpoles from a warm pond

This engraving of a water flea shows its complex anatomy

THE SPAWN IS BORN
As early as January, adult frogs congregrate in ponds and prepare to mate and spawn (pp. 38-9). Around March the female lays up to 3,000 eggs, fertilized by the male, who clings to her back. The water-absorbing jelly around each egg swells, and soon the whole mass is many times her body size.

BIG BROTHERS AND SISTERS
Tadpoles hatch from spawn some two to three weeks after laying. The warmer the water, the faster they develop. Here, common frog tadpoles from a large, cool pond, only two weeks out of their eggs, mingle with four-weekers from a small pond that warmed up more quickly.

Common toad

Dry, warty skin

BORN ON TO THEIR FOOD
Each adult pond snail lays up to 400 eggs, embedded in a jelly-like "rope" attached to the underside of a submerged leaf on which the young snails will feed (p. 52).

A NEW LEAF
In spring water snails lay their eggs under leaves like these water-lily leaves.

Water-lily leaves

Protective jelly

Snail eggs

Pond snails

Water fleas

SPRING BLOOM
Water fleas and other minute animals and plants bring a pea-green soup look to many ponds in spring. This is the early "bloom" of micro-organisms that provides food for larger creature.

TWO SEXES IN ONE
Many adult pond snails are hermaphrodites, having both male and female reproductive organs.

Damage to leaf edge caused by natural splitting

SECOND SPRING
This young water beetle, common in small ponds and ditches, may well be celebrating its second birthday. Two years ago it was an egg, in that autumn a larva, last spring a pupa, and last summer a newly emerged adult.

FIRST SPRING
A water beetle larva has large protrusible jaws ready to tackle and eat any small creature the spring pond has to offer. Some species stay as larvae for two years or more before pupating into adults (p. 51).

KING OF THE BEETLES
The great diving beetle is the king of the carnivores in many small ponds, feeding on tadpoles, small fish and almost anything else it can catch. In fact the dull, furrowed "back" (hard wing covers) on this one indicates it is not a king, but a queen - a female. The male's wing cases are smooth and shiny.

SOME WEEKS TO TAKE-OFF
A mayfly larva displays the characteristic three tails of this group. Despite its name, this larva might become adult and fly off in April or June (p. 50).

Female beetles have furrowed wing covers

Pale-green fronds

Water beetle

Water beetle larva

Erpobdella leech

Mayfly larva

Water slater

Crest along male's back

Male newt

Female newt

Duckweed

LOOKING FOR A WORM
The erpobdella leech loops through the water in search of a meal. This leech does not suck blood, but attacks worms and other soft-bodied small creatures and swallows them whole.

FINDING A MATE
The female water slater piggy-backs the male as he fertilizes the eggs, which she keeps in a pouch under her body.

BREEDING NEWTS
In spring the male newt develops a crest along his back and black spots over his skin. The female's skin remains olive-brown.

GREEN CEILING
In the spring sunshine, duckweed soon spreads across the pond (p. 44). The tiny fronds provide food for snails and insect larvae.

Common frog

Smooth, shiny skin

ONE-YEAR-OLDS
Apart from breeding adults, spawn and tadpoles, you may also find last year's babies around the pond in spring (pp. 38-9).

EARLY FLOWERS
The water crowfoot is an aquatic type of buttercup. The broad, flat leaves that float on the surface shade the water beneath, providing a good hiding place for fish.

Leaves that float on the surface are flat and broad

READY TO MATE
In spring, the male stickleback's throat and underside turn bright red (a red tinge can even be seen from above, as on the male shown here). In this breeding colouration, he entices the female to lay eggs in the nest he has built on the pond bed (p. 25).

Frogs lose their tail soon after emerging

Leaves that grow under water are finely divided

Male stickleback

Female stickleback

Early summer plants

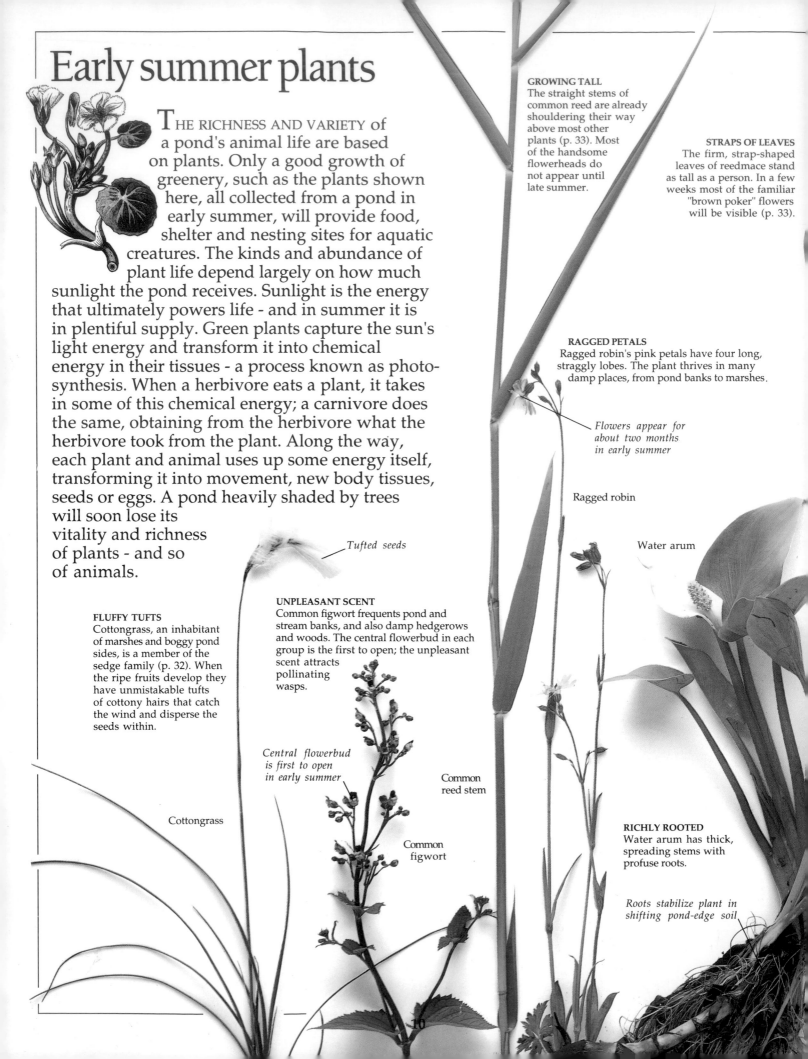

THE RICHNESS AND VARIETY of a pond's animal life are based on plants. Only a good growth of greenery, such as the plants shown here, all collected from a pond in early summer, will provide food, shelter and nesting sites for aquatic creatures. The kinds and abundance of plant life depend largely on how much sunlight the pond receives. Sunlight is the energy that ultimately powers life - and in summer it is in plentiful supply. Green plants capture the sun's light energy and transform it into chemical energy in their tissues - a process known as photosynthesis. When a herbivore eats a plant, it takes in some of this chemical energy; a carnivore does the same, obtaining from the herbivore what the herbivore took from the plant. Along the way, each plant and animal uses up some energy itself, transforming it into movement, new body tissues, seeds or eggs. A pond heavily shaded by trees will soon lose its vitality and richness of plants - and so of animals.

GROWING TALL
The straight stems of common reed are already shouldering their way above most other plants (p. 33). Most of the handsome flowerheads do not appear until late summer.

STRAPS OF LEAVES
The firm, strap-shaped leaves of reedmace stand as tall as a person. In a few weeks most of the familiar "brown poker" flowers will be visible (p. 33).

RAGGED PETALS
Ragged robin's pink petals have four long, straggly lobes. The plant thrives in many damp places, from pond banks to marshes.

Flowers appear for about two months in early summer

Ragged robin

Water arum

Tufted seeds

FLUFFY TUFTS
Cottongrass, an inhabitant of marshes and boggy pond sides, is a member of the sedge family (p. 32). When the ripe fruits develop they have unmistakable tufts of cottony hairs that catch the wind and disperse the seeds within.

UNPLEASANT SCENT
Common figwort frequents pond and stream banks, and also damp hedgerows and woods. The central flowerbud in each group is the first to open; the unpleasant scent attracts pollinating wasps.

Central flowerbud is first to open in early summer

Cottongrass

Common figwort

Common reed stem

RICHLY ROOTED
Water arum has thick, spreading stems with profuse roots.

Roots stabilize plant in shifting pond-edge soil

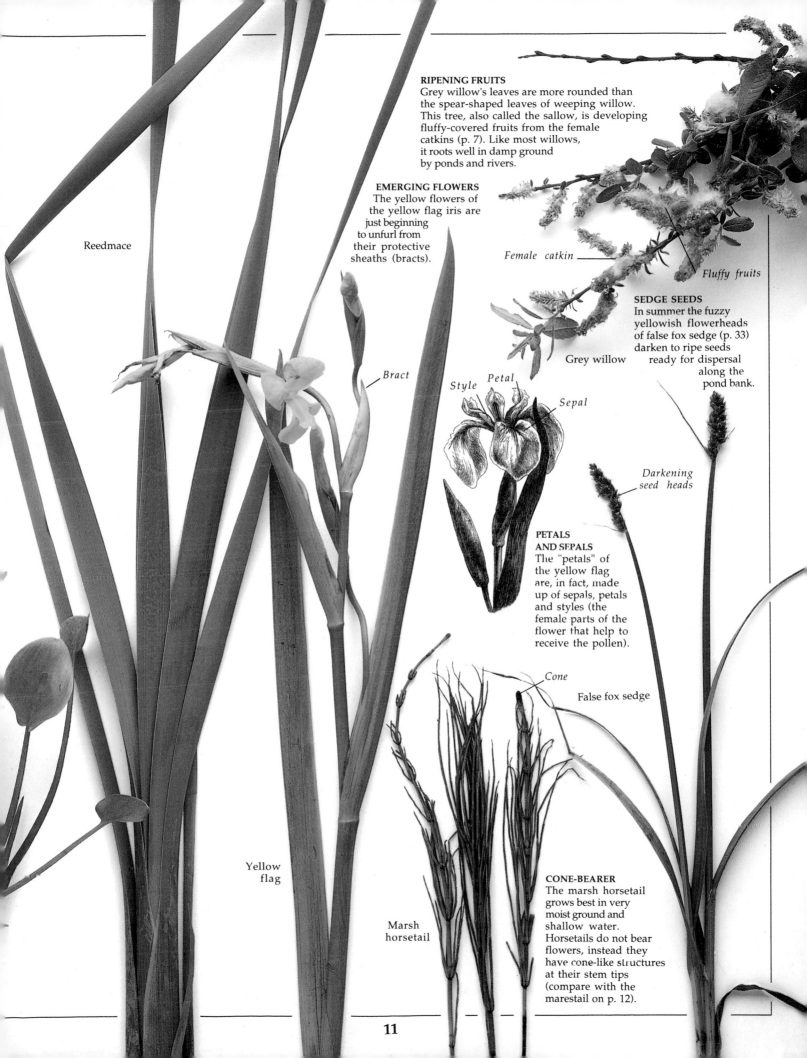

RIPENING FRUITS
Grey willow's leaves are more rounded than the spear-shaped leaves of weeping willow. This tree, also called the sallow, is developing fluffy-covered fruits from the female catkins (p. 7). Like most willows, it roots well in damp ground by ponds and rivers.

EMERGING FLOWERS
The yellow flowers of the yellow flag iris are just beginning to unfurl from their protective sheaths (bracts).

Reedmace

Female catkin

Fluffy fruits

SEDGE SEEDS
In summer the fuzzy yellowish flowerheads of false fox sedge (p. 33) darken to ripe seeds ready for dispersal along the pond bank.

Grey willow

Bract

Style *Petal*

Sepal

Darkening seed heads

PETALS AND SEPALS
The "petals" of the yellow flag are, in fact, made up of sepals, petals and styles (the female parts of the flower that help to receive the pollen).

Cone

False fox sedge

Yellow flag

Marsh horsetail

CONE-BEARER
The marsh horsetail grows best in very moist ground and shallow water. Horsetails do not bear flowers, instead they have cone-like structures at their stem tips (compare with the marestail on p. 12).

Early summer animals

EARLY SUMMER is a time of thinning out and fattening up for pond animals. The swarms of young tadpoles, insect larvae and water snails feed greedily on the abundant plant growth of this season (pp. 10-11). But they are gradually thinned out by larger predatory creatures, such as beetle larvae and dragonfly nymphs (p. 48), newts and small fish. These grow fat and in their turn may fall prey to larger carnivores, from frogs to fish, such as carp and tench, to visiting birds like herons, and perhaps to water shrew, mink and other mammals. And so the food chain of the pond builds up: plants first, then herbivores (plant-eaters), to carnivores (meat-eaters). But this is not the end. Death comes to all and, when it does, creatures such as water slaters move in to consume plant and animal remains. Droppings of all creatures enrich the water, providing minerals and other raw materials for fresh plant growth. So the nutrients go round and round, being recycled in the miniature ecosystem that is the pond.

Silver water beetle, wing cases lifted to show wings

Common toad

GOODBYE FOR THIS YEAR
A few of the dozens of breeding toads may still be hanging about near the pond. But most have now dispersed to their favourite damp corners, in hedges, under logs and among the undergrowth. They will not return to the pond until next spring.

Tadpoles with developing hindlimbs

PETAL-LESS FLOWERS
Marestail is a shallow-water plant of ponds and streams, around whose stems squirm and swim the numerous tiny pond creatures of this season. It bears tiny flowers without petals, where the leaves join the stem.

BACK LEGS FIRST
Frog tadpoles are now fewer in number; many of their siblings have fallen prey to fish, newts, diving beetles and dragonfly nymphs. They have their back legs, which appear after about seven weeks. This change in body shape, from tadpole to adult frog, is called "metamorphosis".

Great pond snail

GROWN UP
This great pond snail is nearing full size, at about 5 cm (2 in) long. It slides slowly over the bottom of the pond, eating decaying plant remains.

Marestail

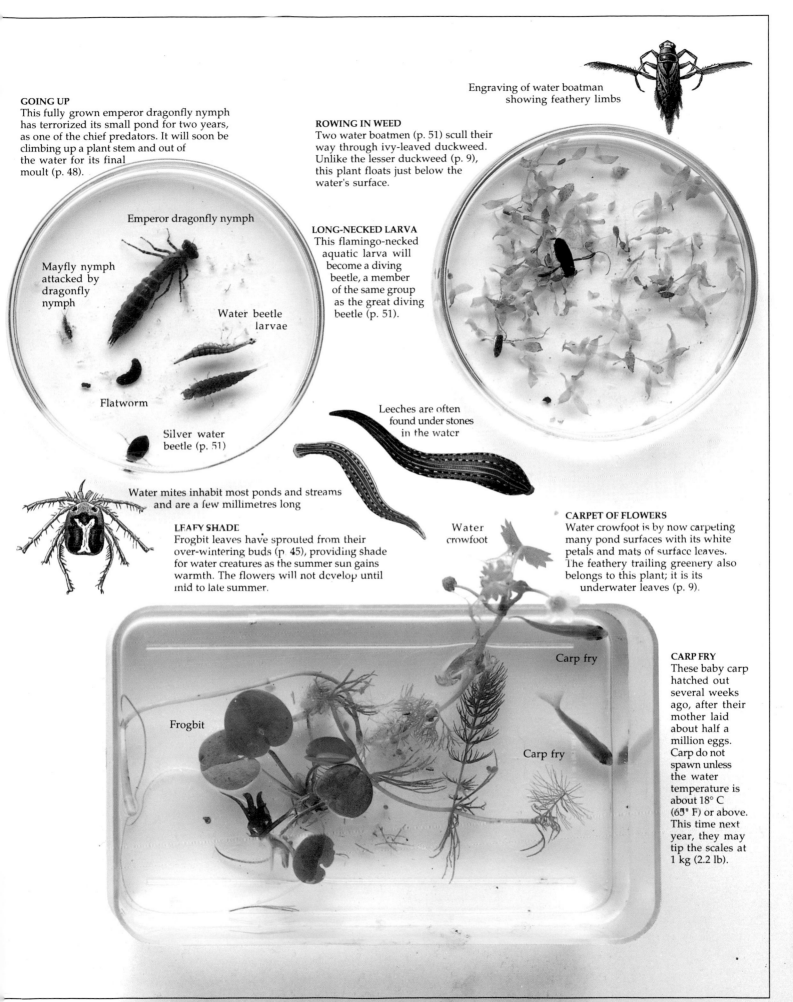

Engraving of water boatman
showing feathery limbs

GOING UP
This fully grown emperor dragonfly nymph
has terrorized its small pond for two years,
as one of the chief predators. It will soon be
climbing up a plant stem and out of
the water for its final
moult (p. 48).

ROWING IN WEED
Two water boatmen (p. 51) scull their
way through ivy-leaved duckweed.
Unlike the lesser duckweed (p. 9),
this plant floats just below the
water's surface.

LONG-NECKED LARVA
This flamingo-necked
aquatic larva will
become a diving
beetle, a member
of the same group
as the great diving
beetle (p. 51).

Emperor dragonfly nymph

Mayfly nymph
attacked by
dragonfly
nymph

Water beetle
larvae

Flatworm

Silver water
beetle (p. 51)

Leeches are often
found under stones
in the water

Water mites inhabit most ponds and streams
and are a few millimetres long

CARPET OF FLOWERS
Water crowfoot is by now carpeting
many pond surfaces with its white
petals and mats of surface leaves.
The feathery trailing greenery also
belongs to this plant; it is its
underwater leaves (p. 9).

LEAFY SHADE
Frogbit leaves have sprouted from their
over-wintering buds (p. 45), providing shade
for water creatures as the summer sun gains
warmth. The flowers will not develop until
mid to late summer.

Water
crowfoot

Carp fry

Frogbit

Carp fry

CARP FRY
These baby carp
hatched out
several weeks
ago, after their
mother laid
about half a
million eggs.
Carp do not
spawn unless
the water
temperature is
about 18° C
(65° F) or above.
This time next
year, they may
tip the scales at
1 kg (2.2 lb).

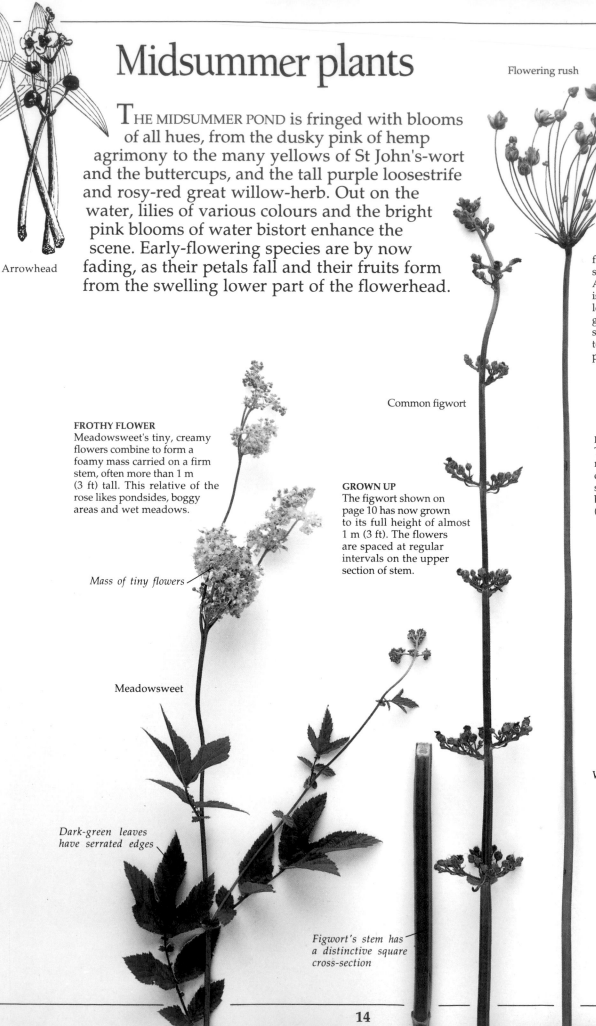

Midsummer plants

THE MIDSUMMER POND is fringed with blooms of all hues, from the dusky pink of hemp agrimony to the many yellows of St John's-wort and the buttercups, and the tall purple loosestrife and rosy-red great willow-herb. Out on the water, lilies of various colours and the bright pink blooms of water bistort enhance the scene. Early-flowering species are by now fading, as their petals fall and their fruits form from the swelling lower part of the flowerhead.

Arrowhead

Flowering rush

Pink flowers on stalks

Developing fruits

RUSH IN BLOOM
The dark pink blooms of flowering rush are borne on stems up to 1.5 m (5 ft) tall. As explained on page 32 this is not a true rush, though its leaves are rush-like and grow in a rosette from the stem base. It is often planted to decorate ornamental ponds.

Common figwort

FROTHY FLOWER
Meadowsweet's tiny, creamy flowers combine to form a foamy mass carried on a firm stem, often more than 1 m (3 ft) tall. This relative of the rose likes pondsides, boggy areas and wet meadows.

Mass of tiny flowers

GROWN UP
The figwort shown on page 10 has now grown to its full height of almost 1 m (3 ft). The flowers are spaced at regular intervals on the upper section of stem.

FRUITS FORMING
The water arum's fruits are ripening as the specialized cup-shaped leaves, called spathes, around them begin to yellow and wither (see also p. 10).

Spathe

Developing fruits

Meadowsweet

Water arum

Dark-green leaves have serrated edges

Figwort's stem has a distinctive square cross-section

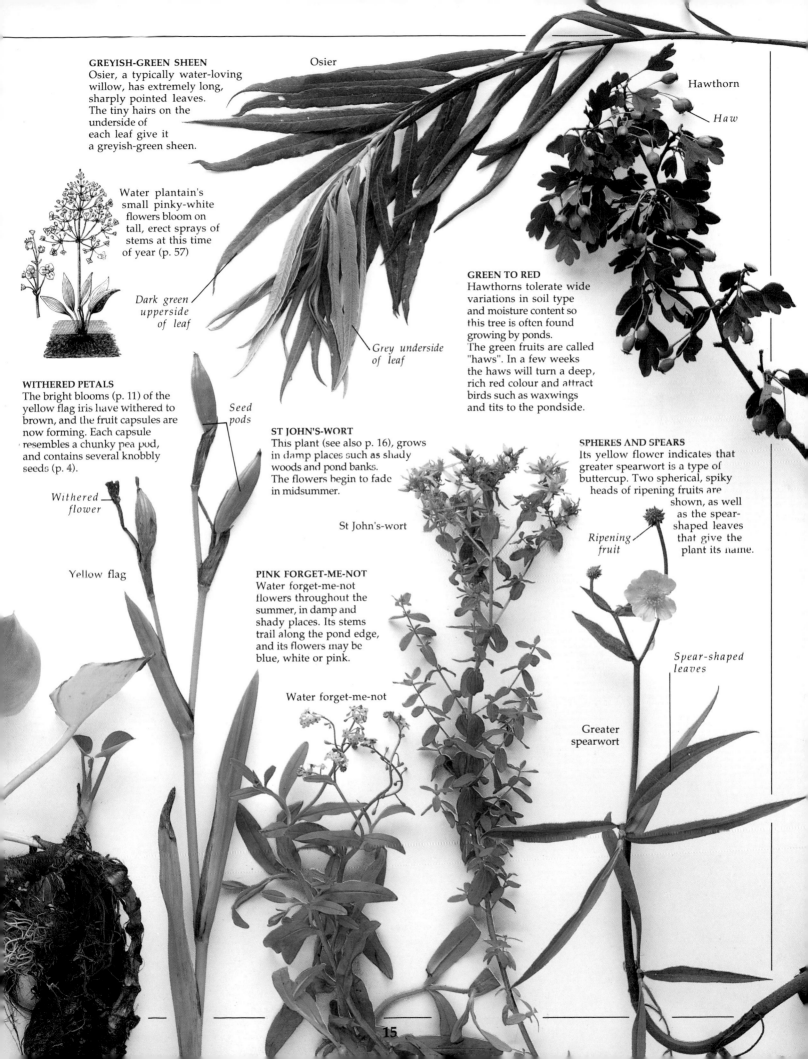

GREYISH-GREEN SHEEN
Osier, a typically water-loving willow, has extremely long, sharply pointed leaves. The tiny hairs on the underside of each leaf give it a greyish-green sheen.

Osier

Hawthorn

Haw

Water plantain's small pinky-white flowers bloom on tall, erect sprays of stems at this time of year (p. 57)

Dark green upperside of leaf

Grey underside of leaf

GREEN TO RED
Hawthorns tolerate wide variations in soil type and moisture content so this tree is often found growing by ponds.
The green fruits are called "haws". In a few weeks the haws will turn a deep, rich red colour and attract birds such as waxwings and tits to the pondside.

WITHERED PETALS
The bright blooms (p. 11) of the yellow flag iris have withered to brown, and the fruit capsules are now forming. Each capsule resembles a chunky pea pod, and contains several knobbly seeds (p. 4).

Seed pods

Withered flower

Yellow flag

ST JOHN'S-WORT
This plant (see also p. 16), grows in damp places such as shady woods and pond banks. The flowers begin to fade in midsummer.

St John's-wort

SPHERES AND SPEARS
Its yellow flower indicates that greater spearwort is a type of buttercup. Two spherical, spiky heads of ripening fruits are shown, as well as the spear-shaped leaves that give the plant its name.

Ripening fruit

PINK FORGET-ME-NOT
Water forget-me-not flowers throughout the summer, in damp and shady places. Its stems trail along the pond edge, and its flowers may be blue, white or pink.

Water forget-me-not

Spear-shaped leaves

Greater spearwort

15

Midsummer animals

MIDSUMMER IS A TIME OF GROWTH and departure in the pond. The frantic spring and early summer rush of new life is quietening. The surviving youngsters of this year's eggs, now fewer in number, settle down to the serious business of growing, laying down food stores and preparing for shorter, colder days ahead. Frog and toad tadpoles have become transformed into air-breathing mini-adults, ready to leave the water and take their first hops on land. A few young newts may stay in gill-sporting tadpole form through the coming autumn and winter, but others, now adult in shape, are also moving away. The exodus from the pond continues as aquatic insect larvae of many kinds develop into adults (p. 50), from tiny gnats, midges and mosquitoes to the mighty dragonflies (p. 48) that prey on them.

Tiny gnats (male and female) dance above the pond's surface during long summer evenings

Water snail

Growth rings

Not rowing but flying, this water boatman shows its strong wings (p. 51)

Toadlet

Newtlets

Gills

Toadlet

NEWTLETS
These young newts still retain their gills, to help absorb oxygen from the warm summer pond water. They hide among weeds, eating water fleas and other tiny creatures.

RINGS AND BANDS
Periods of slow growth are visible on this watersnail's shell. They are the thin rings towards the opening, that cross the spiral banding pattern.

TOADLETS
Toad tadpoles by now have grown their front legs and lost their tails, to resemble their parents. In midsummer they leave the pond for life on land.

HAPPY WANDERER
The wandering snail is more tolerant of soft water (p. 52) than, for example, the great pond snail - and so is more widespread in ponds and slow rivers.

BABY BIVALVES
In about ten years, these young freshwater molluscs will grow many times this size (p. 52). In their early years they are busy feeding and absorbing calcium from the water to build their shell.

SQUARE STEM
There are several species of St John's-wort (p. 15). This is square-stemmed, which lines watersides, marshes and damp hedgerows.

Young freshwater molluscs

Wandering snails

Snail emerging from shell

Square-stemmed St John's-wort

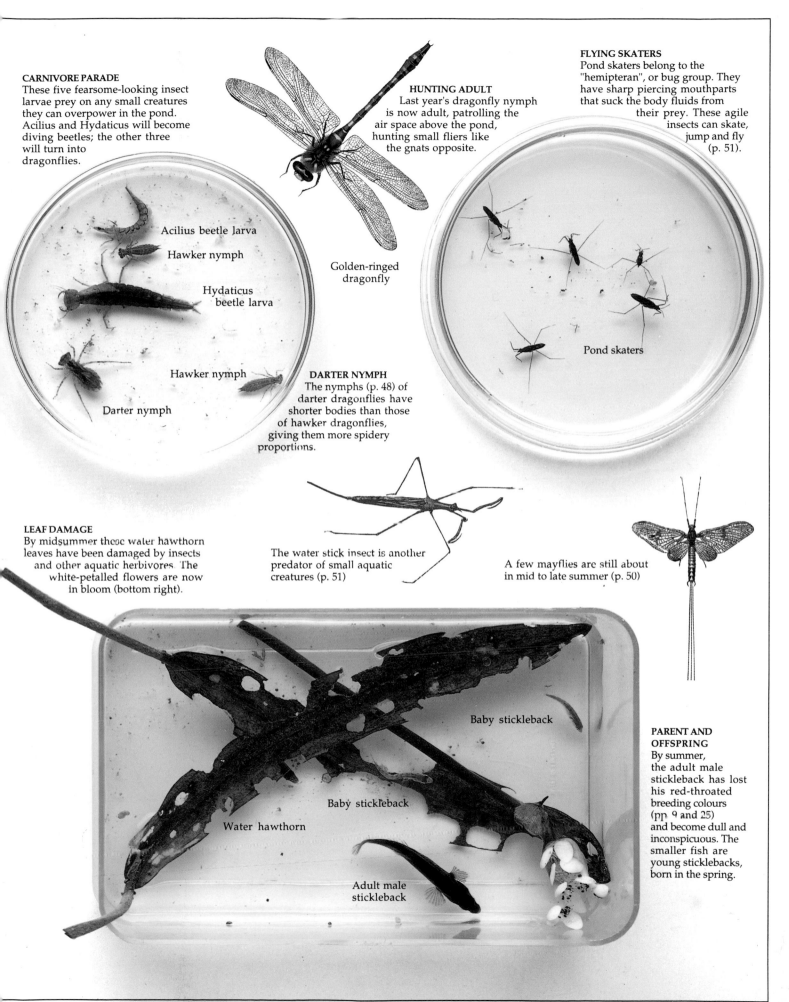

CARNIVORE PARADE
These five fearsome-looking insect larvae prey on any small creatures they can overpower in the pond. Acilius and Hydaticus will become diving beetles; the other three will turn into dragonflies.

HUNTING ADULT
Last year's dragonfly nymph is now adult, patrolling the air space above the pond, hunting small fliers like the gnats opposite.

FLYING SKATERS
Pond skaters belong to the "hemipteran", or bug group. They have sharp piercing mouthparts that suck the body fluids from their prey. These agile insects can skate, jump and fly (p. 51).

Acilius beetle larva

Hawker nymph

Hydaticus beetle larva

Golden-ringed dragonfly

Hawker nymph

DARTER NYMPH
The nymphs (p. 48) of darter dragonflies have shorter bodies than those of hawker dragonflies, giving them more spidery proportions.

Darter nymph

Pond skaters

LEAF DAMAGE
By midsummer these water hawthorn leaves have been damaged by insects and other aquatic herbivores. The white-petalled flowers are now in bloom (bottom right).

The water stick insect is another predator of small aquatic creatures (p. 51)

A few mayflies are still about in mid to late summer (p. 50)

Baby stickleback

PARENT AND OFFSPRING
By summer, the adult male stickleback has lost his red-throated breeding colours (pp. 9 and 25) and become dull and inconspicuous. The smaller fish are young sticklebacks, born in the spring.

Baby stickleback

Water hawthorn

Adult male stickleback

The pond in autumn

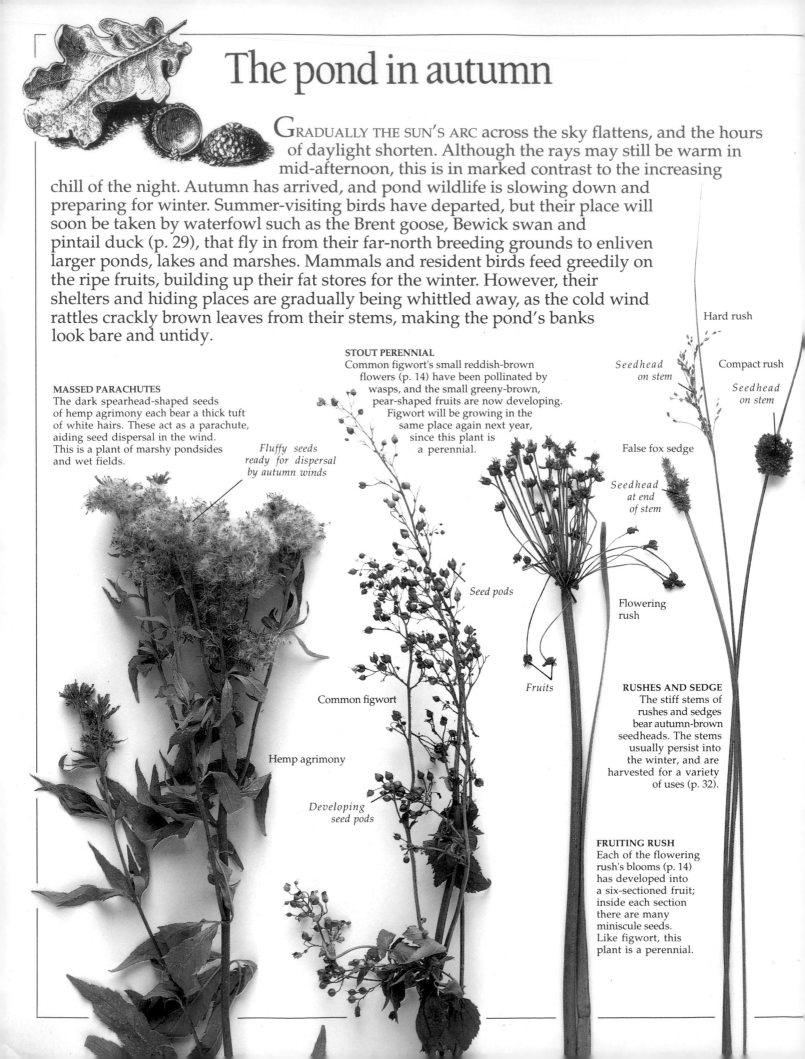

GRADUALLY THE SUN'S ARC across the sky flattens, and the hours of daylight shorten. Although the rays may still be warm in mid-afternoon, this is in marked contrast to the increasing chill of the night. Autumn has arrived, and pond wildlife is slowing down and preparing for winter. Summer-visiting birds have departed, but their place will soon be taken by waterfowl such as the Brent goose, Bewick swan and pintail duck (p. 29), that fly in from their far-north breeding grounds to enliven larger ponds, lakes and marshes. Mammals and resident birds feed greedily on the ripe fruits, building up their fat stores for the winter. However, their shelters and hiding places are gradually being whittled away, as the cold wind rattles crackly brown leaves from their stems, making the pond's banks look bare and untidy.

MASSED PARACHUTES
The dark spearhead-shaped seeds of hemp agrimony each bear a thick tuft of white hairs. These act as a parachute, aiding seed dispersal in the wind. This is a plant of marshy pondsides and wet fields.

Fluffy seeds ready for dispersal by autumn winds

STOUT PERENNIAL
Common figwort's small reddish-brown flowers (p. 14) have been pollinated by wasps, and the small greeny-brown, pear-shaped fruits are now developing. Figwort will be growing in the same place again next year, since this plant is a perennial.

Seed pods

Common figwort

Hemp agrimony

Developing seed pods

Fruits

Hard rush

Seedhead on stem

Compact rush

Seedhead on stem

False fox sedge

Seedhead at end of stem

Flowering rush

RUSHES AND SEDGE
The stiff stems of rushes and sedges bear autumn-brown seedheads. The stems usually persist into the winter, and are harvested for a variety of uses (p. 32).

FRUITING RUSH
Each of the flowering rush's blooms (p. 14) has developed into a six-sectioned fruit; inside each section there are many miniscule seeds. Like figwort, this plant is a perennial.

WINTER POKER
Reedmace's familiar brown "poker" of seeds stands guard over marshes and ponds, usually throughout the winter. In spring the poker bursts to scatter the fluffy-haired seeds.

Brown "poker" full of seeds

SNAILS SLOWING DOWN
Falling water temperatures mean that even pond snails begin to move about more slowly, tending to stay in deeper water.

Pond snails

Reedmace

Newtlet

Dragonfly nymph

Caddis fly cases

Alder

Alder cones

ALDER "CONES"
In autumn the alder's green fruits ripen to a browny-black colour and stay on the tree during winter. They are sometimes mistaken for small pine cones, but the alder is not a conifer. It prefers pond banks and streamsides, and its light seeds drop onto the water and float to new ground.

HOME IN A TUBE
Rectangular leaf fragments stuck into a spiral pattern and curled into a tube, signal the larval case of the great red sedge, a type of caddis fly (p. 50). These larvae will emerge as adult flies next year.

Seed pods

Yellow flag

NEXT YEAR'S ADULT
Dragonfly nymphs found in the pond at this time of year will overwinter and emerge next year.

AUTUMN JUVENILE
A young common newt, still equipped with gills, will overwinter as a "juvenile", and finish its transformation into an adult next year.

RECYCLING FUNGI
Animal and plant corpses are digested by fungi and their nutrients made available for recycling. Here, an old pondside tree was attacked and weakened by bracket fungi.

Bracket fungi grow on the outside of the trunk

ON THE BOTTOM
Leaves, twigs and other debris blow into the pond, or are washed in by heavy autumn rains. This accumulation of debris, overlying the mud of the pond bed, will shelter all manner of small water creatures during the winter months.

SOON TO SET SEED
The seed capsules of the yellow flag iris are now thick with ripening brown seeds (compare the same "pods" on p. 15). Eventually the fleshy capsule walls dry out and split into three boat-shaped segments; these peel back to release the seeds (p. 4).

Oak leaf

Willow leaf

Birch leaf

Willow twigs

The pond in winter

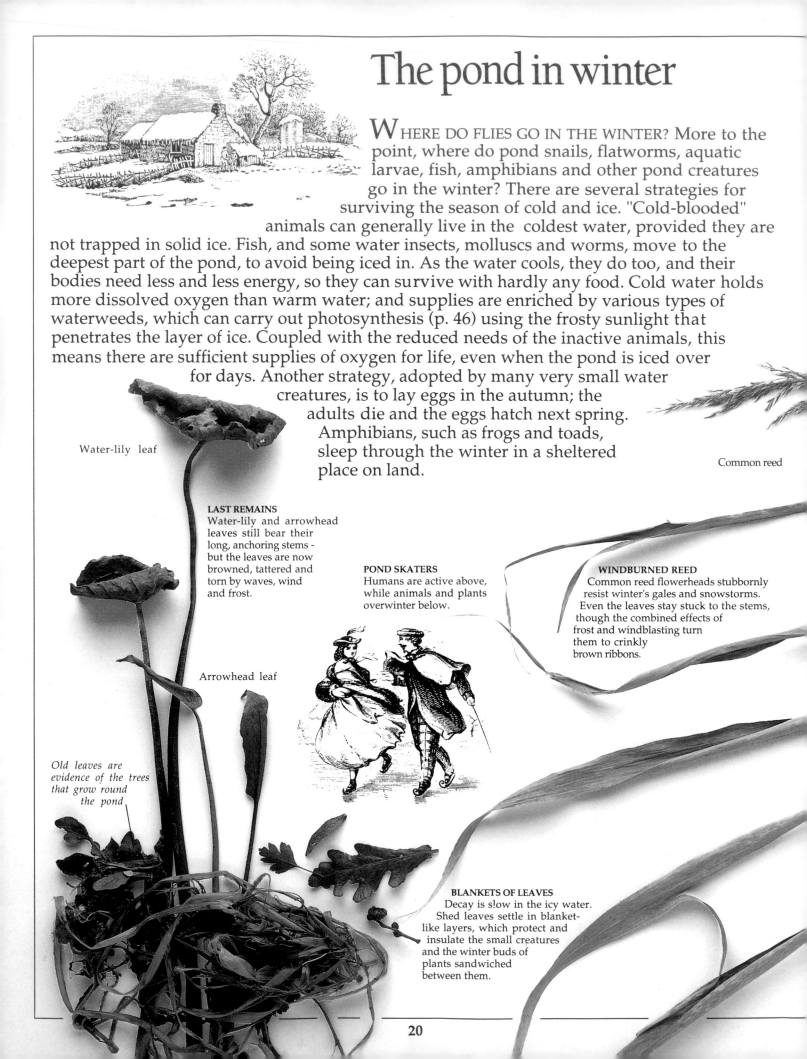

WHERE DO FLIES GO IN THE WINTER? More to the point, where do pond snails, flatworms, aquatic larvae, fish, amphibians and other pond creatures go in the winter? There are several strategies for surviving the season of cold and ice. "Cold-blooded" animals can generally live in the coldest water, provided they are not trapped in solid ice. Fish, and some water insects, molluscs and worms, move to the deepest part of the pond, to avoid being iced in. As the water cools, they do too, and their bodies need less and less energy, so they can survive with hardly any food. Cold water holds more dissolved oxygen than warm water; and supplies are enriched by various types of waterweeds, which can carry out photosynthesis (p. 46) using the frosty sunlight that penetrates the layer of ice. Coupled with the reduced needs of the inactive animals, this means there are sufficient supplies of oxygen for life, even when the pond is iced over for days. Another strategy, adopted by many very small water creatures, is to lay eggs in the autumn; the adults die and the eggs hatch next spring. Amphibians, such as frogs and toads, sleep through the winter in a sheltered place on land.

Water-lily leaf

Common reed

LAST REMAINS
Water-lily and arrowhead leaves still bear their long, anchoring stems - but the leaves are now browned, tattered and torn by waves, wind and frost.

POND SKATERS
Humans are active above, while animals and plants overwinter below.

WINDBURNED REED
Common reed flowerheads stubbornly resist winter's gales and snowstorms. Even the leaves stay stuck to the stems, though the combined effects of frost and windblasting turn them to crinkly brown ribbons.

Arrowhead leaf

Old leaves are evidence of the trees that grow round the pond

BLANKETS OF LEAVES
Decay is slow in the icy water. Shed leaves settle in blanket-like layers, which protect and insulate the small creatures and the winter buds of plants sandwiched between them.

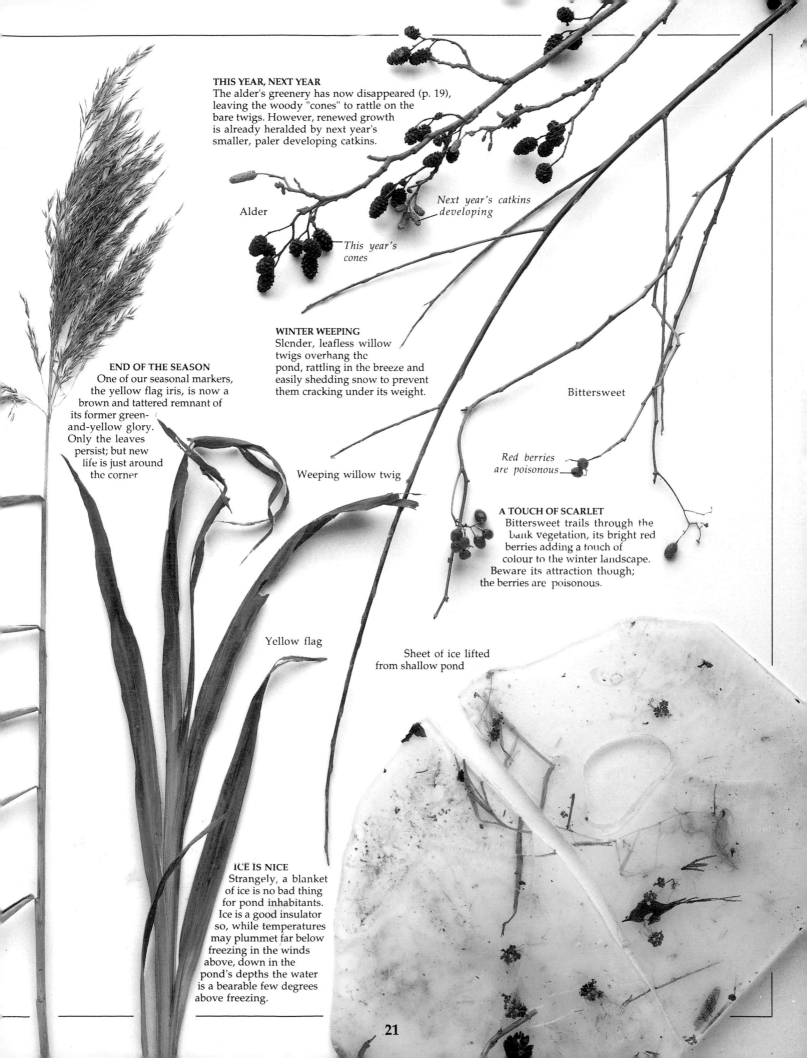

THIS YEAR, NEXT YEAR
The alder's greenery has now disappeared (p. 19), leaving the woody "cones" to rattle on the bare twigs. However, renewed growth is already heralded by next year's smaller, paler developing catkins.

Alder

Next year's catkins developing

This year's cones

WINTER WEEPING
Slender, leafless willow twigs overhang the pond, rattling in the breeze and easily shedding snow to prevent them cracking under its weight.

Bittersweet

Red berries are poisonous

END OF THE SEASON
One of our seasonal markers, the yellow flag iris, is now a brown and tattered remnant of its former green-and-yellow glory. Only the leaves persist; but new life is just around the corner

Weeping willow twig

A TOUCH OF SCARLET
Bittersweet trails through the bank vegetation, its bright red berries adding a touch of colour to the winter landscape. Beware its attraction though; the berries are poisonous.

Yellow flag

Sheet of ice lifted from shallow pond

ICE IS NICE
Strangely, a blanket of ice is no bad thing for pond inhabitants. Ice is a good insulator so, while temperatures may plummet far below freezing in the winds above, down in the pond's depths the water is a bearable few degrees above freezing.

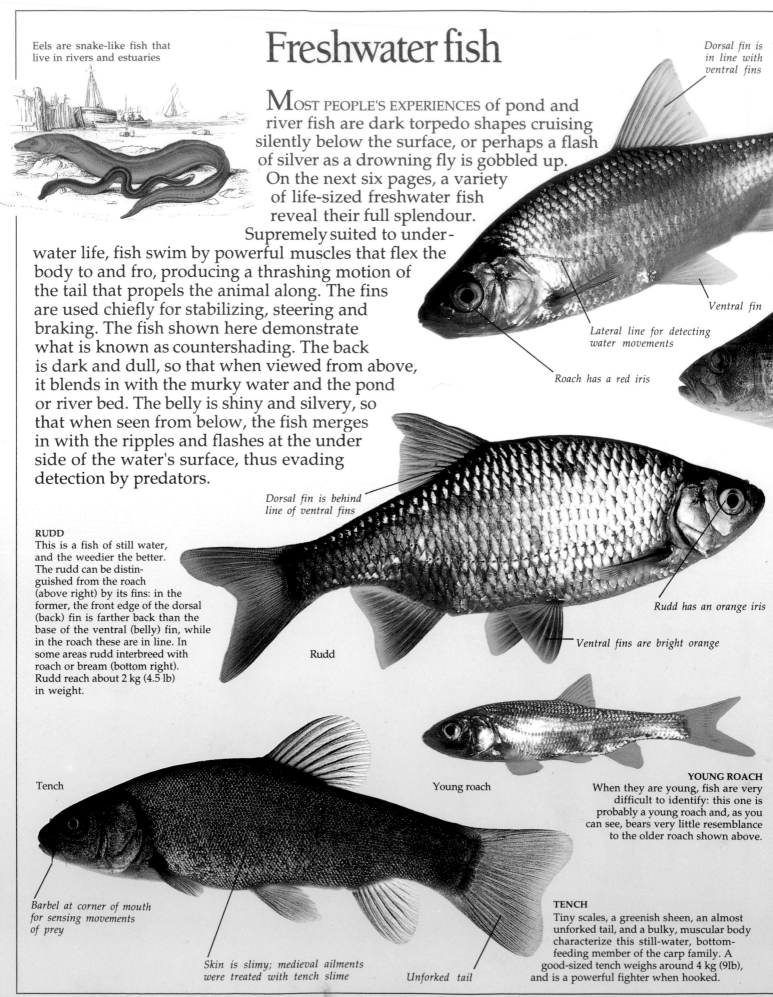

Freshwater fish

Eels are snake-like fish that live in rivers and estuaries

MOST PEOPLE'S EXPERIENCES of pond and river fish are dark torpedo shapes cruising silently below the surface, or perhaps a flash of silver as a drowning fly is gobbled up. On the next six pages, a variety of life-sized freshwater fish reveal their full splendour. Supremely suited to under-water life, fish swim by powerful muscles that flex the body to and fro, producing a thrashing motion of the tail that propels the animal along. The fins are used chiefly for stabilizing, steering and braking. The fish shown here demonstrate what is known as countershading. The back is dark and dull, so that when viewed from above, it blends in with the murky water and the pond or river bed. The belly is shiny and silvery, so that when seen from below, the fish merges in with the ripples and flashes at the under side of the water's surface, thus evading detection by predators.

Dorsal fin is in line with ventral fins

Ventral fin

Lateral line for detecting water movements

Roach has a red iris

RUDD

This is a fish of still water, and the weedier the better. The rudd can be distin-guished from the roach (above right) by its fins: in the former, the front edge of the dorsal (back) fin is farther back than the base of the ventral (belly) fin, while in the roach these are in line. In some areas rudd interbreed with roach or bream (bottom right). Rudd reach about 2 kg (4.5 lb) in weight.

Dorsal fin is behind line of ventral fins

Rudd

Rudd has an orange iris

Ventral fins are bright orange

Young roach

YOUNG ROACH
When they are young, fish are very difficult to identify: this one is probably a young roach and, as you can see, bears very little resemblance to the older roach shown above.

Tench

Barbel at corner of mouth for sensing movements of prey

Skin is slimy; medieval ailments were treated with tench slime

Unforked tail

TENCH
Tiny scales, a greenish sheen, an almost unforked tail, and a bulky, muscular body characterize this still-water, bottom-feeding member of the carp family. A good-sized tench weighs around 4 kg (9lb), and is a powerful fighter when hooked.

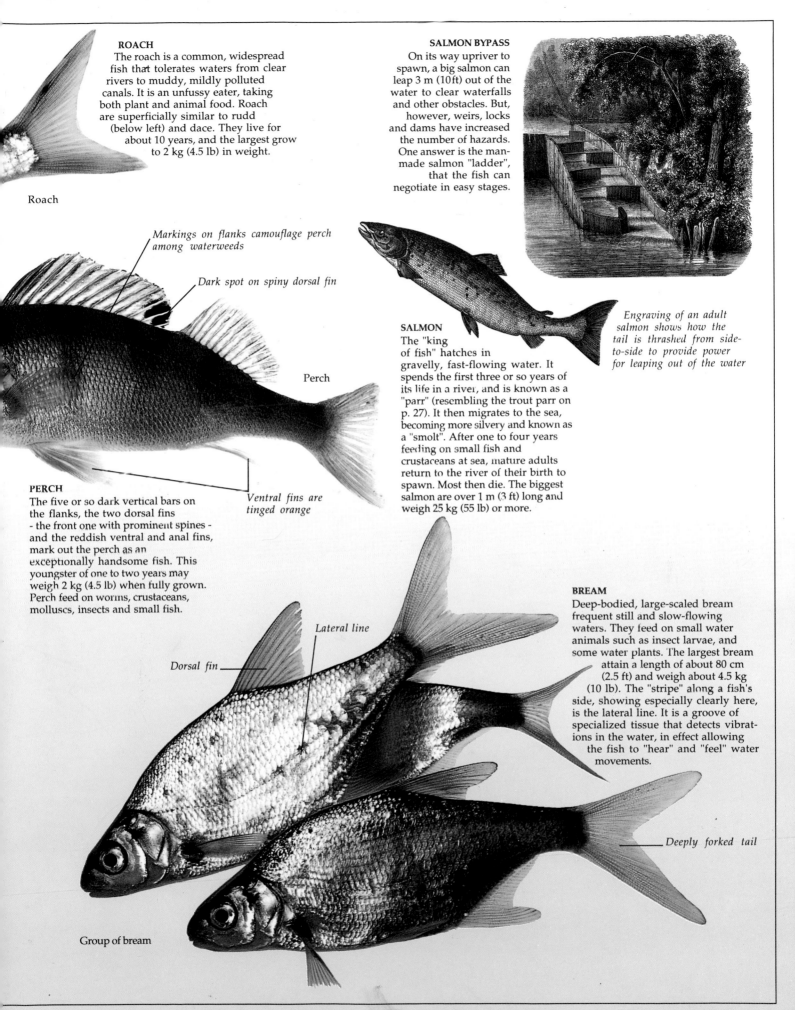

ROACH

The roach is a common, widespread fish that tolerates waters from clear rivers to muddy, mildly polluted canals. It is an unfussy eater, taking both plant and animal food. Roach are superficially similar to rudd (below left) and dace. They live for about 10 years, and the largest grow to 2 kg (4.5 lb) in weight.

Roach

SALMON BYPASS

On its way upriver to spawn, a big salmon can leap 3 m (10 ft) out of the water to clear waterfalls and other obstacles. But, however, weirs, locks and dams have increased the number of hazards. One answer is the man-made salmon "ladder", that the fish can negotiate in easy stages.

Markings on flanks camouflage perch among waterweeds

Dark spot on spiny dorsal fin

Perch

SALMON

The "king of fish" hatches in gravelly, fast-flowing water. It spends the first three or so years of its life in a river, and is known as a "parr" (resembling the trout parr on p. 27). It then migrates to the sea, becoming more silvery and known as a "smolt". After one to four years feeding on small fish and crustaceans at sea, mature adults return to the river of their birth to spawn. Most then die. The biggest salmon are over 1 m (3 ft) long and weigh 25 kg (55 lb) or more.

Engraving of an adult salmon shows how the tail is thrashed from side-to-side to provide power for leaping out of the water

PERCH

The five or so dark vertical bars on the flanks, the two dorsal fins - the front one with prominent spines - and the reddish ventral and anal fins, mark out the perch as an exceptionally handsome fish. This youngster of one to two years may weigh 2 kg (4.5 lb) when fully grown. Perch feed on worms, crustaceans, molluscs, insects and small fish.

Ventral fins are tinged orange

BREAM

Deep-bodied, large-scaled bream frequent still and slow-flowing waters. They feed on small water animals such as insect larvae, and some water plants. The largest bream attain a length of about 80 cm (2.5 ft) and weigh about 4.5 kg (10 lb). The "stripe" along a fish's side, showing especially clearly here, is the lateral line. It is a groove of specialized tissue that detects vibrations in the water, in effect allowing the fish to "hear" and "feel" water movements.

Lateral line

Dorsal fin

Deeply forked tail

Group of bream

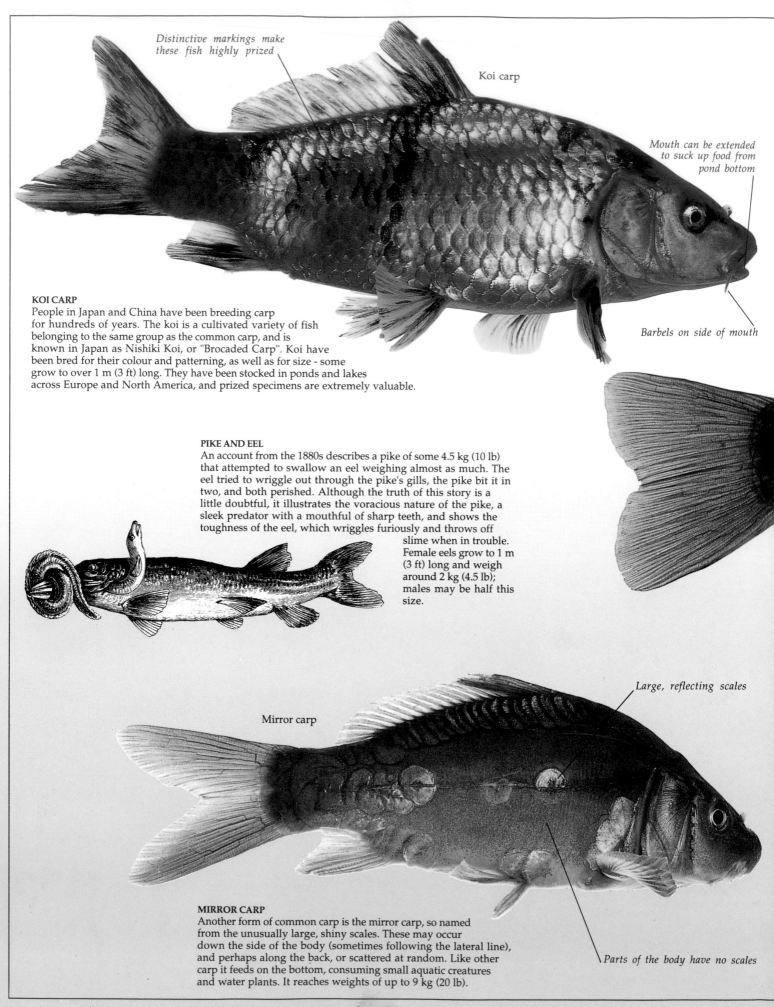

Distinctive markings make these fish highly prized

Koi carp

Mouth can be extended to suck up food from pond bottom

KOI CARP
People in Japan and China have been breeding carp
for hundreds of years. The koi is a cultivated variety of fish
belonging to the same group as the common carp, and is
known in Japan as Nishiki Koi, or "Brocaded Carp". Koi have
been bred for their colour and patterning, as well as for size - some
grow to over 1 m (3 ft) long. They have been stocked in ponds and lakes
across Europe and North America, and prized specimens are extremely valuable.

Barbels on side of mouth

PIKE AND EEL
An account from the 1880s describes a pike of some 4.5 kg (10 lb)
that attempted to swallow an eel weighing almost as much. The
eel tried to wriggle out through the pike's gills, the pike bit it in
two, and both perished. Although the truth of this story is a
little doubtful, it illustrates the voracious nature of the pike, a
sleek predator with a mouthful of sharp teeth, and shows the
toughness of the eel, which wriggles furiously and throws off
slime when in trouble.
Female eels grow to 1 m
(3 ft) long and weigh
around 2 kg (4.5 lb);
males may be half this
size.

Large, reflecting scales

Mirror carp

MIRROR CARP
Another form of common carp is the mirror carp, so named
from the unusually large, shiny scales. These may occur
down the side of the body (sometimes following the lateral line),
and perhaps along the back, or scattered at random. Like other
carp it feeds on the bottom, consuming small aquatic creatures
and water plants. It reaches weights of up to 9 kg (20 lb).

Parts of the body have no scales

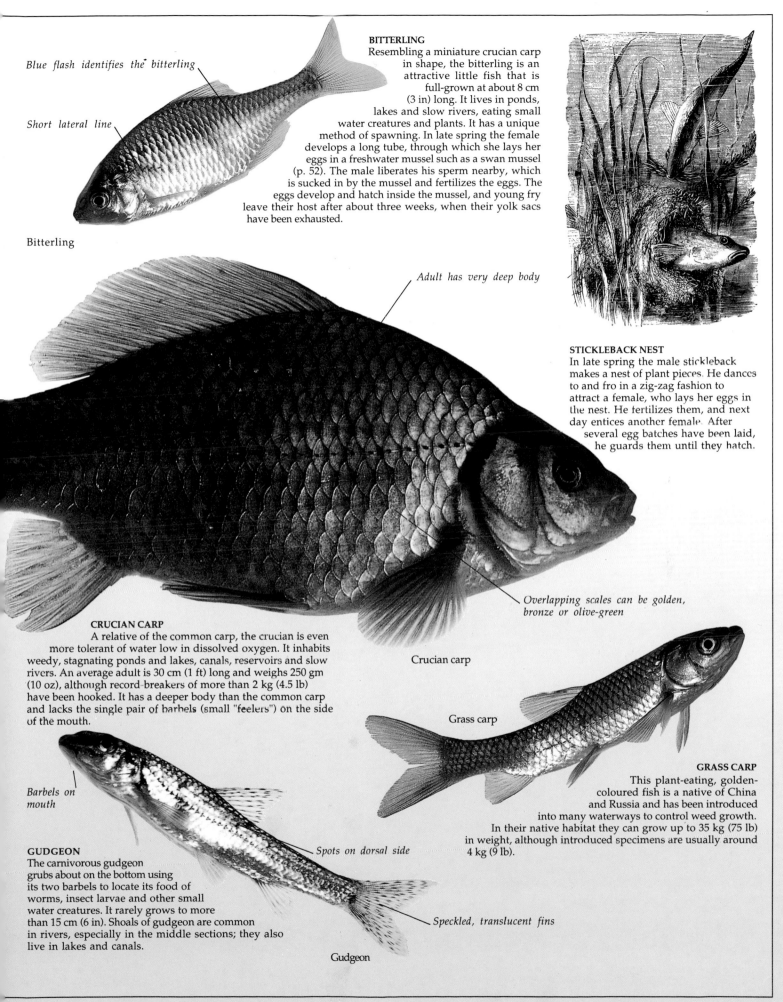

Blue flash identifies the bitterling

Short lateral line

Bitterling

BITTERLING
Resembling a miniature crucian carp in shape, the bitterling is an attractive little fish that is full-grown at about 8 cm (3 in) long. It lives in ponds, lakes and slow rivers, eating small water creatures and plants. It has a unique method of spawning. In late spring the female develops a long tube, through which she lays her eggs in a freshwater mussel such as a swan mussel (p. 52). The male liberates his sperm nearby, which is sucked in by the mussel and fertilizes the eggs. The eggs develop and hatch inside the mussel, and young fry leave their host after about three weeks, when their yolk sacs have been exhausted.

STICKLEBACK NEST
In late spring the male stickleback makes a nest of plant pieces. He dances to and fro in a zig-zag fashion to attract a female, who lays her eggs in the nest. He fertilizes them, and next day entices another female. After several egg batches have been laid, he guards them until they hatch.

Adult has very deep body

Overlapping scales can be golden, bronze or olive-green

Crucian carp

CRUCIAN CARP
A relative of the common carp, the crucian is even more tolerant of water low in dissolved oxygen. It inhabits weedy, stagnating ponds and lakes, canals, reservoirs and slow rivers. An average adult is 30 cm (1 ft) long and weighs 250 gm (10 oz), although record-breakers of more than 2 kg (4.5 lb) have been hooked. It has a deeper body than the common carp and lacks the single pair of barbels (small "feelers") on the side of the mouth.

Grass carp

GRASS CARP
This plant-eating, golden-coloured fish is a native of China and Russia and has been introduced into many waterways to control weed growth. In their native habitat they can grow up to 35 kg (75 lb) in weight, although introduced specimens are usually around 4 kg (9 lb).

Barbels on mouth

GUDGEON
The carnivorous gudgeon grubs about on the bottom using its two barbels to locate its food of worms, insect larvae and other small water creatures. It rarely grows to more than 15 cm (6 in). Shoals of gudgeon are common in rivers, especially in the middle sections; they also live in lakes and canals.

Spots on dorsal side

Speckled, translucent fins

Gudgeon

The trout

FEW FRESHWATER FISH match the trout for natural beauty and grace, for fighting power when hooked - and for taste when cooked! Trout belong to the salmon family. The brown trout and sea trout are, in fact, different forms of the same species. The former lives all its life in fresh water; the latter feeds in the sea and enters its home stream in summer, to breed in autumn. Adult brown trout may approach 1 m (3 ft) in length, while sea trout can be half as long again. There are many intermediates between these two forms, and distinguishing between them is difficult, as sea trout darken when they have been in fresh water for a few weeks and resemble the brown trout. In any case, trout vary enormously in appearance, depending on where they live, the nature of the water, the type of stream or lake bed, and the food they eat. Rainbow trout are another trout species altogether.

TYPICAL TROUT COUNTRY
An ideal trout stream - clear and cool running water, high in dissolved oxygen, with a gravelly bed for spawning. Trout are also found in clean lakes, usually in the shallows near their food.

Lateral line

Movements of the very mobile pectoral fins enable the fish to swim upwards or downwards

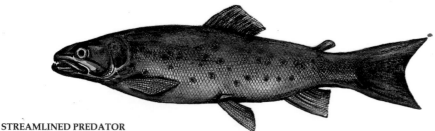

STREAMLINED PREDATOR
Brown trout, like other trout, are carnivorous. Food varies from tiny water fleas, flies, aquatic insect larvae (such as caddis larvae) and freshwater shrimps, to shellfish and other molluscs. The big "ferox" brown trout, from large, deep lakes, prey on other fish such as char or whitefish.

Brown trout

COLOURS OF THE RAINBOW
Rainbow trout were originally found in western North America (especially California). Like the brown trout, there are sea, lake and river forms. Their eggs were brought to Europe in the 1910s, and these fish have since been introduced into many rivers, reservoirs and lakes, to provide sport for anglers and food. Rainbow trout breed in some large reservoirs, but rivers have to be regularly stocked with young produced on "trout farms". The rainbow trout can live in warmer, less oxygenated water than the brown trout, so they are stocked in small lakes and large ponds where the brown trout would probably not survive.

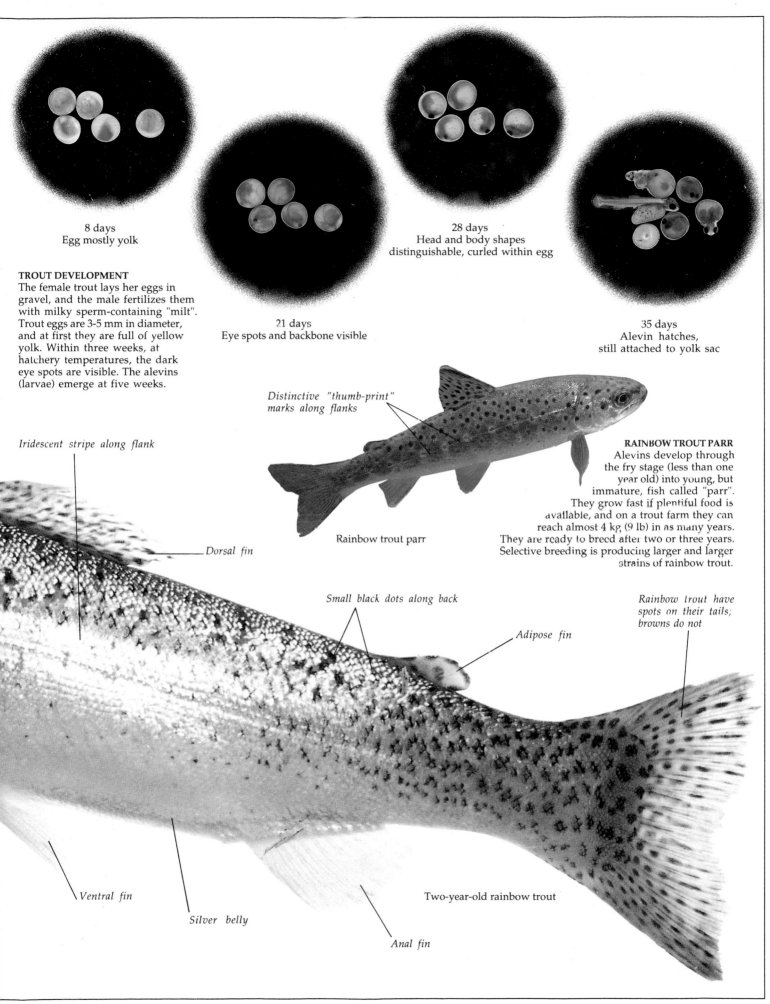

8 days
Egg mostly yolk

21 days
Eye spots and backbone visible

28 days
Head and body shapes
distinguishable, curled within egg

35 days
Alevin hatches,
still attached to yolk sac

TROUT DEVELOPMENT

The female trout lays her eggs in gravel, and the male fertilizes them with milky sperm-containing "milt". Trout eggs are 3-5 mm in diameter, and at first they are full of yellow yolk. Within three weeks, at hatchery temperatures, the dark eye spots are visible. The alevins (larvae) emerge at five weeks.

Distinctive "thumb-print"
marks along flanks

RAINBOW TROUT PARR

Alevins develop through the fry stage (less than one year old) into young, but immature, fish called "parr". They grow fast if plentiful food is available, and on a trout farm they can reach almost 4 kg (9 lb) in as many years. They are ready to breed after two or three years. Selective breeding is producing larger and larger strains of rainbow trout.

Rainbow trout parr

Iridescent stripe along flank

Dorsal fin

Small black dots along back

Adipose fin

Rainbow trout have
spots on their tails;
browns do not

Ventral fin

Silver belly

Anal fin

Two-year-old rainbow trout

Waterfowl

WATER AND ITS RESIDENT WILDLIFE attracts an amazing variety of birds. Quite at home on ponds, lakes and rivers (as well as seashores) across the world are about 150 species of wildfowl, including swans, geese and ducks. These generally heavy-bodied birds have webbed feet for swimming, and long, mobile necks for dabbling in the water and rummaging in the muddy bed for food. During spring, the dense bank vegetation provides many species with safe and sheltered nesting sites. In summer, the proud parents can be seen leading their fluffy chicks across the water. Aquatic plants and animals are a ready source of food for most of the year. In winter, when ponds freeze over, many wildfowl retreat to parks and gardens where they feast on scraps donated by well-wishing humans. Others fly south, often covering vast distances to find a more favourable climate in which to spend the winter.

Eider duck nest
and eggs

*Soft down feathers insulate
the eggs in the nest*

Teal nest and eggs

SPECIALLY GROWN DOWN
Ultra-soft eiderdown feathers grow on the female eider duck's breast. She plucks them to cocoon her eggs as she nests on sea or lake shore or river bank.

TEAL NEST
The teal makes its nest in dense undergrowth. The female is very careful when visiting her chicks, so as not to attract predators.

TUFTED DUCK EGG
The six to 14 eggs are laid in a nest close to the water's edge. The chick hatches after 25 days in the egg, and within a day it is swimming.

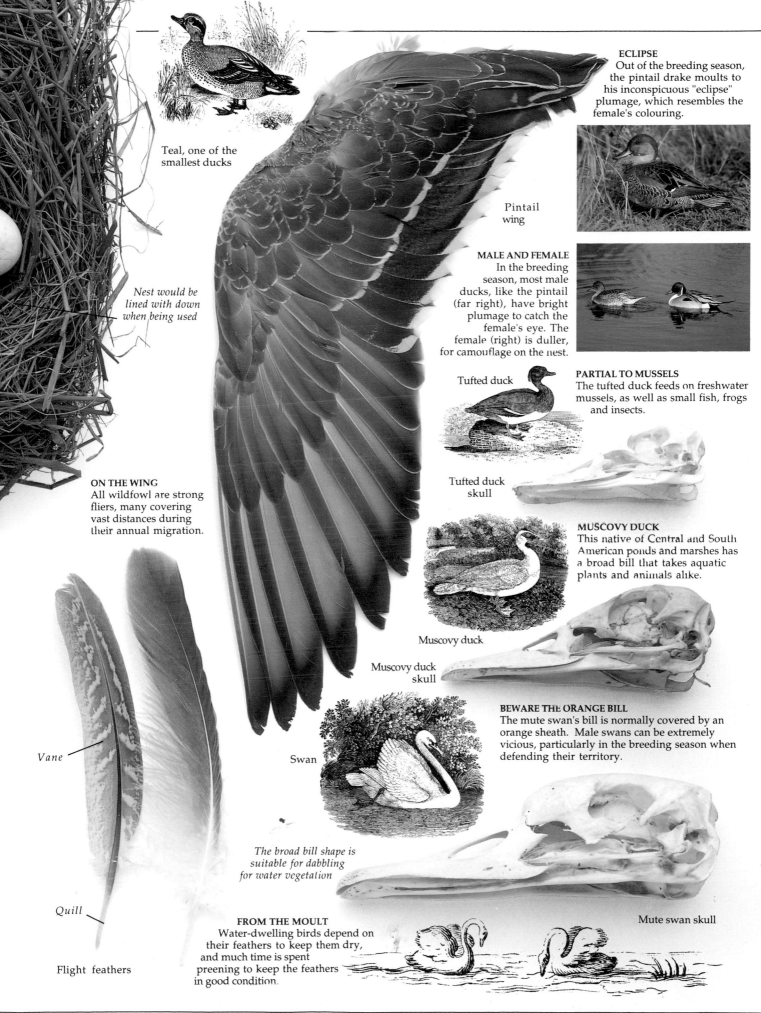

Teal, one of the
smallest ducks

Nest would be
lined with down
when being used

ON THE WING
All wildfowl are strong
fliers, many covering
vast distances during
their annual migration.

Vane

Quill

Flight feathers

FROM THE MOULT
Water-dwelling birds depend on
their feathers to keep them dry,
and much time is spent
preening to keep the feathers
in good condition.

Pintail
wing

Swan

*The broad bill shape is
suitable for dabbling
for water vegetation*

ECLIPSE
Out of the breeding season,
the pintail drake moults to
his inconspicuous "eclipse"
plumage, which resembles the
female's colouring.

MALE AND FEMALE
In the breeding
season, most male
ducks, like the pintail
(far right), have bright
plumage to catch the
female's eye. The
female (right) is duller,
for camouflage on the nest.

Tufted duck

PARTIAL TO MUSSELS
The tufted duck feeds on freshwater
mussels, as well as small fish, frogs
and insects.

Tufted duck
skull

MUSCOVY DUCK
This native of Central and South
American ponds and marshes has
a broad bill that takes aquatic
plants and animals alike.

Muscovy duck

Muscovy duck
skull

BEWARE THE ORANGE BILL
The mute swan's bill is normally covered by an
orange sheath. Male swans can be extremely
vicious, particularly in the breeding season when
defending their territory.

Mute swan skull

Waterbirds

Kingfisher

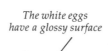

A STRETCH OF WATER acts as a magnet for all types of bird life. Many species, from sparrows to pheasants, come to drink. Others come to feed, from the tall, elegant heron that stands motionless as it watches for prey, to the flash of shimmering blue that signifies a kingfisher diving for its dinner. Bank plants, floating and submerged waterweeds, fish, frogs, insect larvae, shellfish and other aquatic life provide food for many birds. Some species, like reed buntings and warblers, find security in the impenetrable reed beds and dense waterside vegetation. Here they nest and raise their chicks, safe from predators such as foxes and hawks.

Kingfisher wing

THE EXPERT ANGLER
The brilliantly coloured kingfisher dives from its favourite perch for fish, tadpoles and shellfish. The broadsword-shaped bill is ideal for stabbing or spearing fish, then holding the slippery prey until it can be beaten into stillness on a branch and swallowed headfirst.

The white eggs have a glossy surface

Kingfisher eggs

KINGFISHER WING AND TAIL
The electric colours act as a warning to predatory birds, advertizing that the flesh is foul-tasting.

Tail and wing markings vary from species to species

Short wings beat rapidly when flying

Kingfisher tail

Kingfisher skull

Sharp bill for stabbing fish

WHITE EGGS
Kingfishers nest in a streambank burrow up to 1 m (3 ft) long, hence the white eggs - no need for camouflaging colours.

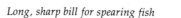

Long, sharp bill for spearing fish

Heron skull

Heron

LONG AND LANKY
Herons inhabit ponds, marshes and rivers, stalking fish and frogs in the shallows.

HERON'S HARPOON
The heron's fearsome bill makes an excellent fish-stabbing spear. This bird stands patiently until prey comes within reach, then darts out its long neck, stabs the victim, tosses it round and swallows it whole.

Bittern skull

BITTERN
This bird points its bill skywards and sways with the reeds to avoid detection. It can also climb up reed stems. The bittern builds a shallow platform of reed leaves and stalks, hidden deep in the reed beds. The five to six eggs take four weeks to hatch.

STEALTHY STALKER
The bittern is a solitary, daytime feeder, using its pointed bill to catch frogs, small fish and insects.

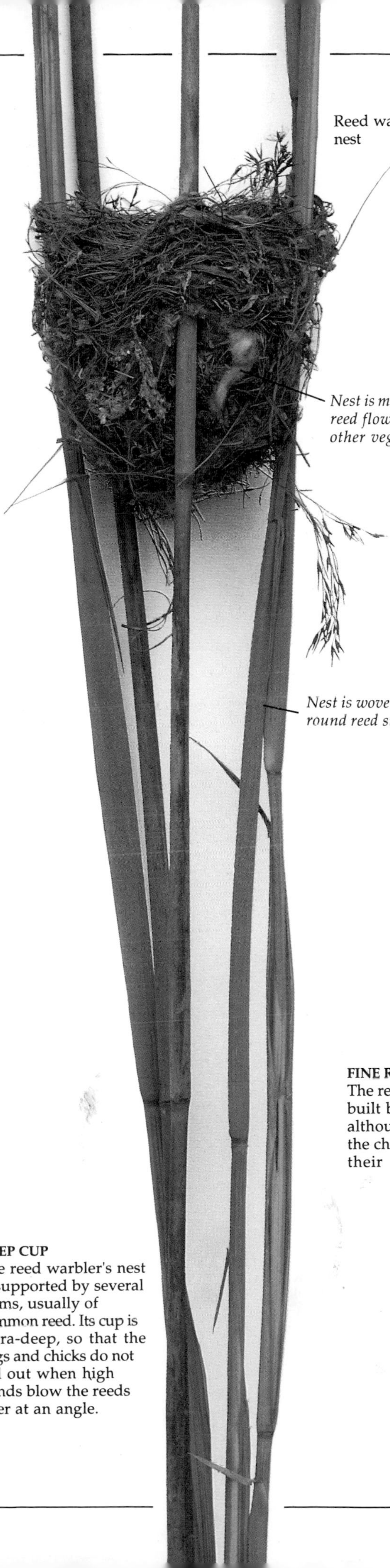

Reed warbler nest

Nest is made from reed flowerheads and other vegetation

Nest is woven round reed stalks

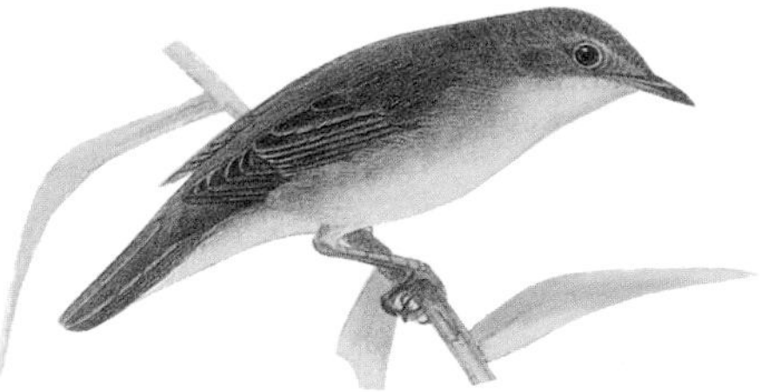

Reed warbler

WARNING All the eggs shown here come from established museum collections. Collecting or handling wild birds' eggs is now illegal.

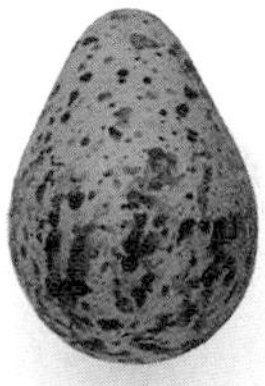

SNIPE EGG
The colouring camouflages the eggs in the nest of this small wading bird.

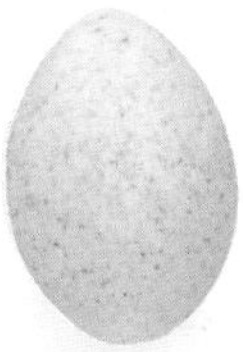

LITTLE GREBE EGG
White when laid, eggs get discoloured by plants and mud. The little grebe is also known as the "dabchick".

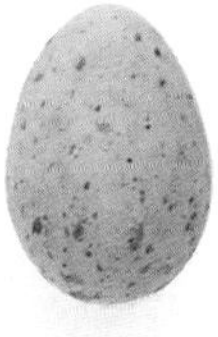

WATER RAIL EGG
Water rails are shy birds of waterside undergrowth. There can be as many as 15 eggs in a clutch.

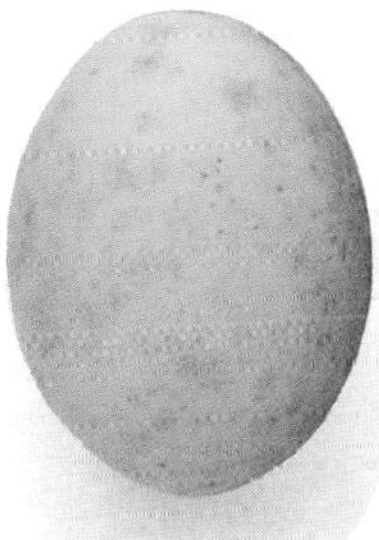

HERON EGG
The blue eggs are laid in well-defended nests built of sticks and twigs.

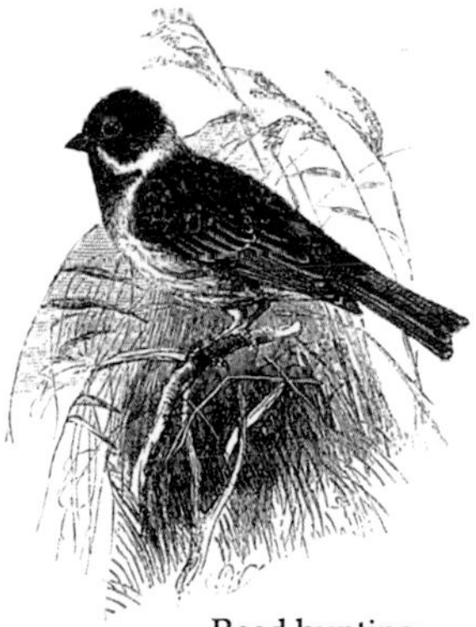

Reed bunting

FINE RUSHWORK
The reed bunting's nest is built by the female alone, although both parents feed the chicks on insects and their larvae.

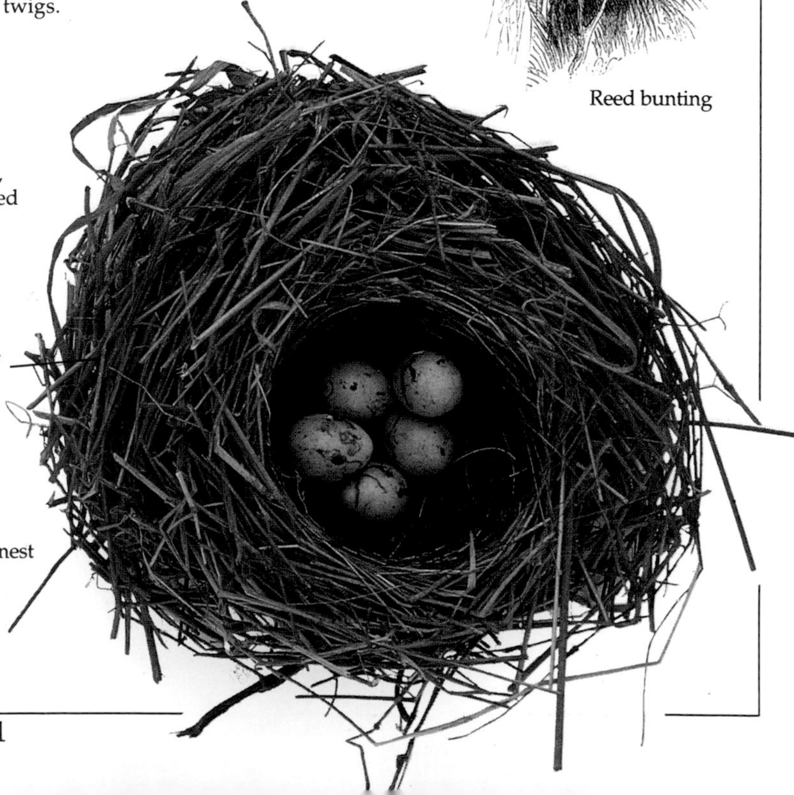

The nest is made of grasses and moss

Reed bunting nest

DEEP CUP
The reed warbler's nest is supported by several stems, usually of common reed. Its cup is extra-deep, so that the eggs and chicks do not fall out when high winds blow the reeds over at an angle.

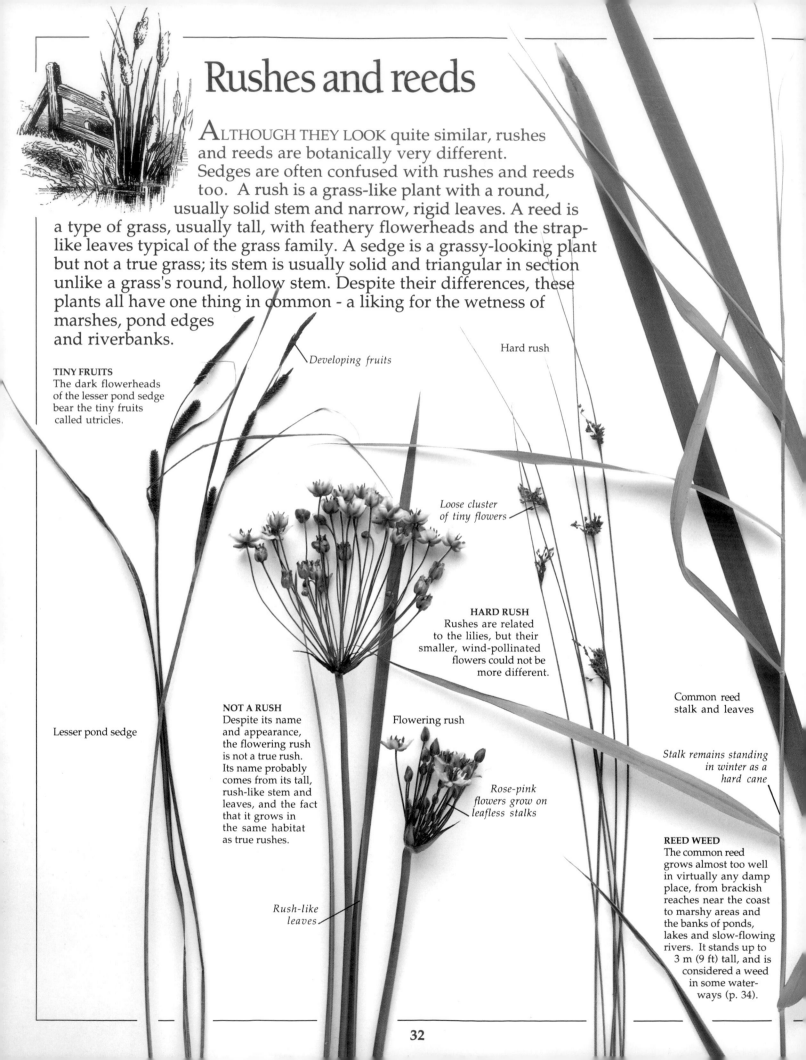

Rushes and reeds

ALTHOUGH THEY LOOK quite similar, rushes and reeds are botanically very different. Sedges are often confused with rushes and reeds too. A rush is a grass-like plant with a round, usually solid stem and narrow, rigid leaves. A reed is a type of grass, usually tall, with feathery flowerheads and the strap-like leaves typical of the grass family. A sedge is a grassy-looking plant but not a true grass; its stem is usually solid and triangular in section unlike a grass's round, hollow stem. Despite their differences, these plants all have one thing in common - a liking for the wetness of marshes, pond edges and riverbanks.

Developing fruits

Hard rush

TINY FRUITS
The dark flowerheads of the lesser pond sedge bear the tiny fruits called utricles.

Loose cluster of tiny flowers

HARD RUSH
Rushes are related to the lilies, but their smaller, wind-pollinated flowers could not be more different.

Lesser pond sedge

NOT A RUSH
Despite its name and appearance, the flowering rush is not a true rush. Its name probably comes from its tall, rush-like stem and leaves, and the fact that it grows in the same habitat as true rushes.

Flowering rush

Common reed stalk and leaves

Stalk remains standing in winter as a hard cane

Rose-pink flowers grow on leafless stalks

REED WEED
The common reed grows almost too well in virtually any damp place, from brackish reaches near the coast to marshy areas and the banks of ponds, lakes and slow-flowing rivers. It stands up to 3 m (9 ft) tall, and is considered a weed in some water-ways (p. 34).

Rush-like leaves

Male flowers release
clouds of pollen

Female flowers are
fertilized by wind-
carried pollen from
male flowers and
fluffy seeds are
released when the
flowerhead splits
open

Ten to 20 male
flowerheads

Branched
bur-reed

Two to four
female
flowerheads

Male and
female flowers
in the same
flowerhead

Great
reedmace

BRANCHING OUT
Each stem of branched
bur-reed bears both male
and female flowers.
The smaller, ball-shaped
ones towards the tip
are male; the female
ones are larger and
spiky, rather like
a rolled-up
hedgehog.

False fox sedge

Triangular stem
has sharp edges
if rubbed
downwards

Branched bur-reed

FALSE FOX SEDGE
On top of sharp-edged
stems sit the tufty,
yellow-green flowerheads
containing both male and
female flowers.

Flower
stalk

TWO HEADS IN ONE
The great reedmace's
poker-shaped flowerhead
is in two parts. Above are
hundreds of golden
pollen-bearing male organs,
and below are thousands of
tiny female flowers packed
into the brown cigar-shape.
The whole resembles the mace,
a weapon of medieval knights,
hence the name. The plant is
commonly, but wrongly, called
the bulrush, after the painting
of *Moses in the Bulrushes* (p. 35).

Bract at base of
each branch of
flower stalk

33

The reed bed

THE REED BED IS THE SILENT INVADER OF OPEN WATER. Dense growths of tall, marshy-ground plants, such as reedmace and common reed, spread around the pond's edge by thick underground stems (rhizomes). These grow sideways through the mud towards the water and send up fresh shoots at intervals. They spread into the shallows, pushing aside water-lilies and marestails. The strong new reed stems slow any water movements and trap current-borne particles. At the end of each season the old leaves, stems and fruits add to the accumulating tangle. Within a few years previously open water can be turned into thickly vegetated marsh. Some years later the reed bed has moved on, still swallowing up the shallows, and drier-ground plants such as osiers and sallows (types of willow) have moved in at the back of the bed. This conversion of water to land by characteristic stages is an example of "ecological succession".

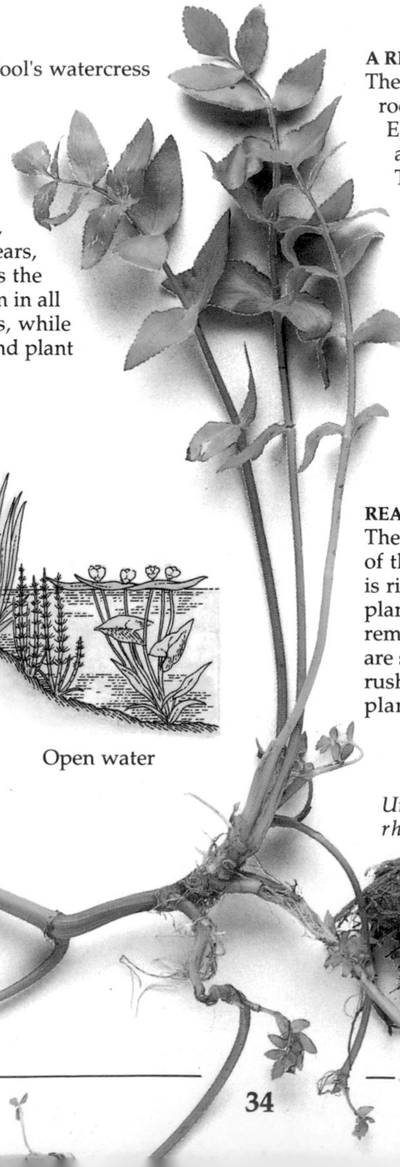

WATER TO DRY LAND

Shown below are characteristic plants of pond and lake edge, with sallows and sedges higher up the shore, reed beds towards the middle, and marestails and long-stemmed lilies in deeper water. As the reeds spread and invade the water, this becomes clogged and marshy and, over the years, the whole pattern of plant growth moves towards the centre of the pond. Of course, this does not happen in all bodies of water. People clear or harvest the reeds, while feeding animals, storms, flood currents and plant diseases keep a natural balance.

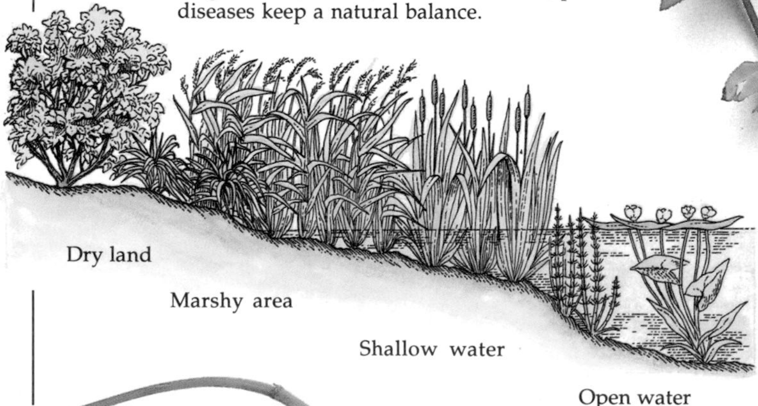

Fool's watercress

Dry land

Marshy area

Shallow water

Open water

A REED ROOF OVER THEIR HEADS

The strong, long-persisting reeds are used as roofing material in many regions, from huts in Egypt and Sudan, to houses on stilts in Indonesia, and wooden cabins in southern North America. The English thatch style (above) offers excellent rain-repelling and insulating features.

A skilled thatcher working with quality reeds can make a roof that remains weatherproof for 40 years or more.

CREEPING CRESS

The fool's watercress gets its name because its leaves resemble true watercress. It is found in large quantities at the back of many reed beds, its horizontal, straggling stems adding to the general tangle of vegetation.

READY FOR RECYCLING

The thick, black mud of the reed-bed areas is rich in decaying plant and animal remains. Its nutrients are soon recycled by the rushes, reeds and other plants.

Reed-bed mud

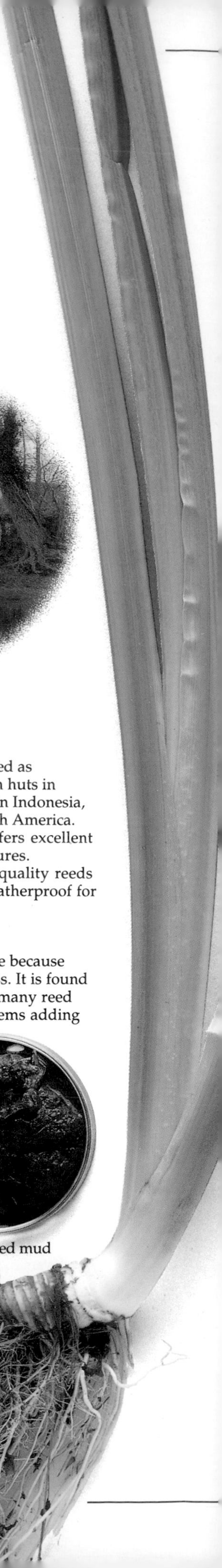

Underground rhizome

Horizontal stems

Sweet flag   *Long straight stalks*

Flowerhead may be 2.5 m (8 ft) above the roots

Dark-greeen leaves have pale undersides

EARLY HARVEST
The reed cutter's season is usually the tail-end of winter and early spring. Last year's stems are cut near the base, before this year's shoots emerge, so ensuring a future harvest.

THICK AND FLESHY
The juicy, strap-shaped leaves of sweet flag sprout from a thick horizontal stem, itself bearing many small roots which help in the process of binding the glutinous marshy mud.

Osier shoot

The thin leaves dry very quickly when picked

Top of common reed stem

MOSES IN THE . . . ?
As a baby, Moses was supposedly hidden in a basket in a reed bed on the Nile's banks to avoid detection. Illustrations showing this are titled *Moses in the Bulrushes* although most versions portray the baby in a clump of reedmace. This confusion has led to the name "bulrush" being popularly applied to reedmace (p. 33); the true bulrush resembling in general form the spike rush.

WILLOWS FOR WEAVING
Osiers are found at the back of reed beds, on less marshy ground. They have long, straight shoots and a shrubby shape. They are often coppiced (cut at ground level) to provide pliant stems ("withies") for woven chairs and baskets.

THE STRAIGHT AND NARROW
The straight, narrow stems of common reed are ideal thatching material. They are also used to make paper and other pulp-based materials. Plant growth in reed beds is often relatively fast, with plenty of water and nutrients, and slender stems and leaves that allow light to penetrate to the lower levels.

Base of common reed stem

Waterside mammals

FRESHWATER HABITATS, from rivers and streams to the marshy edges of lakes and ponds, provide a home and food for a number of mammals. All the "aquatic" mammals shown here have fur coats adapted to their watery habitat. The fur of a mink, for example, is of two main types. Long, thick, flattened "guard hairs" provide physical protection and camouflaging colouration. For each guard hair there are 20 or more softer hairs of the underfur, only half as long, which trap air to keep water out and body heat in. The owners sensibly spend much time combing and cleaning their fur, keeping it in tip-top condition. Another adaptation for watery life is webs between the toes, for more efficient swimming.

FURRY FORAGER
The water shrew's dark-furred body is only about 9 cm (3 in) long. This bustling insectivore often lives in a bankside system of narrow tunnels that press water from its coat as it squeezes through. It eats small fish, water insects and even frogs, and forages on dry land for worms and other small creatures.

Mink

ADAPTABLE CARNIVORE
Minks are less specialized hunters than otters and, besides fish, will take birds, aquatic insects and land animals such as rabbits. The broad, webbed back feet provide the main swimming power.

American mink skull

Canine teeth

Molar teeth

TOOTHLESS "BEAK"
When a baby platypus hatches it has teeth, but these are soon lost. Adults grind up the food of shellfish, water insects and worms using horny plates along their jaws.

TEARERS AND SHEARERS
The mink's four long canine teeth, towards the front of its mouth, are built for catching prey and tearing flesh. The molars, at the back, are ridged for shearing.

Platypus

Platypus skull

Elongated bill for grinding food

DUCK'S BILL, MAMMAL'S FUR
The Australian platypus, a monotreme (egg-laying mammal) has a "bill" covered with leathery, sensitive skin. The bill is its only means of detecting food, by touch, as it forages in muddy creek beds. It closes its eyes and ears when diving.

LODGE IN THE RIVER
A beaver family lives in a semi-submerged mud-and-stick house called a "lodge". The beavers build a dam of branches, twigs, stones and mud across the stream, which raises the local water level and isolates the lodge for safety. During winter they swim under the ice to a "deep freezer" food cache of woody stems and twigs.

Lodge

Mud-and-stick walls

Living chamber (above water)

Food store

Raised water level

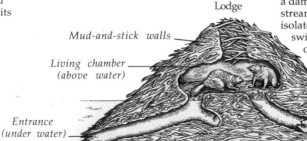

Dam

Entrance (under water)

Long canine teeth for grasping fish

Otter skull

WATCHFUL SWIMMER
Nostrils, eyes and ears are placed high on the head, so that the otter can swim almost submerged yet still breathe, look and listen.

HUNTING THE OTTER
Otter hunting was once considered a sport, and still occurs in some places, although in many countries this animal is now protected by law. Today these creatures are also at risk from development of waterways for angling and leisure pursuits, and from pollution.

THE GAME OF LIFE
Otters spend much time at play, either on their own or with one another. Such "games" may help to sharpen hunting skills.

Molar teeth for grinding food

ENORMOUS GNAWERS
The beaver's large chisel-like front teeth (typical of rodents) can gnaw through tree trunks with ease.

NATURE'S LOGGERS
Beavers cut down trees for food and also to build homes in lakes they create for themselves (below left). They eat waterweeds, leaves and other plant matter.

Large incisor teeth for gnawing

Beaver skull

Beaver

FLAT SLAP
The beaver's tail is flattened and scaly. Besides its use as a rudder and paddle, it can be slapped onto the water's surface to warn colleagues of danger.

Beaver tail

Frogs, toads and newts

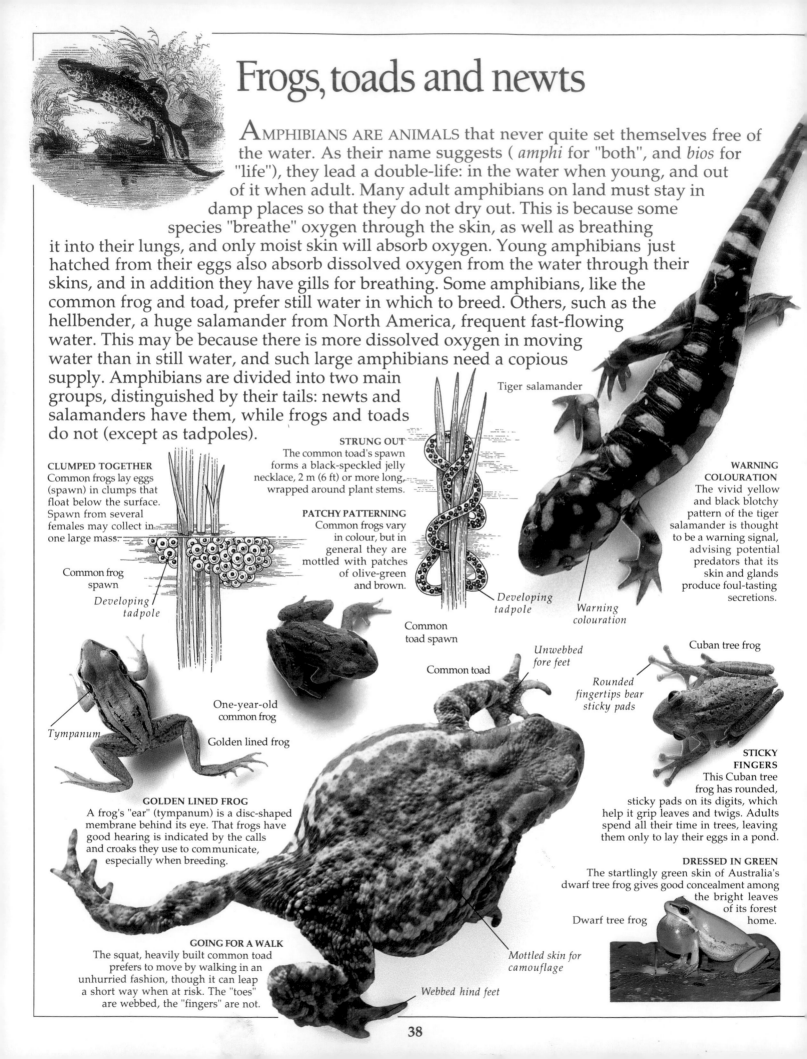

AMPHIBIANS ARE ANIMALS that never quite set themselves free of the water. As their name suggests (*amphi* for "both", and *bios* for "life"), they lead a double-life: in the water when young, and out of it when adult. Many adult amphibians on land must stay in damp places so that they do not dry out. This is because some species "breathe" oxygen through the skin, as well as breathing it into their lungs, and only moist skin will absorb oxygen. Young amphibians just hatched from their eggs also absorb dissolved oxygen from the water through their skins, and in addition they have gills for breathing. Some amphibians, like the common frog and toad, prefer still water in which to breed. Others, such as the hellbender, a huge salamander from North America, frequent fast-flowing water. This may be because there is more dissolved oxygen in moving water than in still water, and such large amphibians need a copious supply. Amphibians are divided into two main groups, distinguished by their tails: newts and salamanders have them, while frogs and toads do not (except as tadpoles).

Tiger salamander

CLUMPED TOGETHER
Common frogs lay eggs (spawn) in clumps that float below the surface. Spawn from several females may collect in one large mass.

Common frog spawn

Developing tadpole

STRUNG OUT
The common toad's spawn forms a black-speckled jelly necklace, 2 m (6 ft) or more long, wrapped around plant stems.

PATCHY PATTERNING
Common frogs vary in colour, but in general they are mottled with patches of olive-green and brown.

Developing tadpole

Common toad spawn

WARNING COLOURATION
The vivid yellow and black blotchy pattern of the tiger salamander is thought to be a warning signal, advising potential predators that its skin and glands produce foul-tasting secretions.

Warning colouration

Unwebbed fore feet

Common toad

Cuban tree frog

Rounded fingertips bear sticky pads

One-year-old common frog

Tympanum

Golden lined frog

GOLDEN LINED FROG
A frog's "ear" (tympanum) is a disc-shaped membrane behind its eye. That frogs have good hearing is indicated by the calls and croaks they use to communicate, especially when breeding.

STICKY FINGERS
This Cuban tree frog has rounded, sticky pads on its digits, which help it grip leaves and twigs. Adults spend all their time in trees, leaving them only to lay their eggs in a pond.

DRESSED IN GREEN
The startlingly green skin of Australia's dwarf tree frog gives good concealment among the bright leaves of its forest home.

Dwarf tree frog

GOING FOR A WALK
The squat, heavily built common toad prefers to move by walking in an unhurried fashion, though it can leap a short way when at risk. The "toes" are webbed, the "fingers" are not.

Mottled skin for camouflage

Webbed hind feet

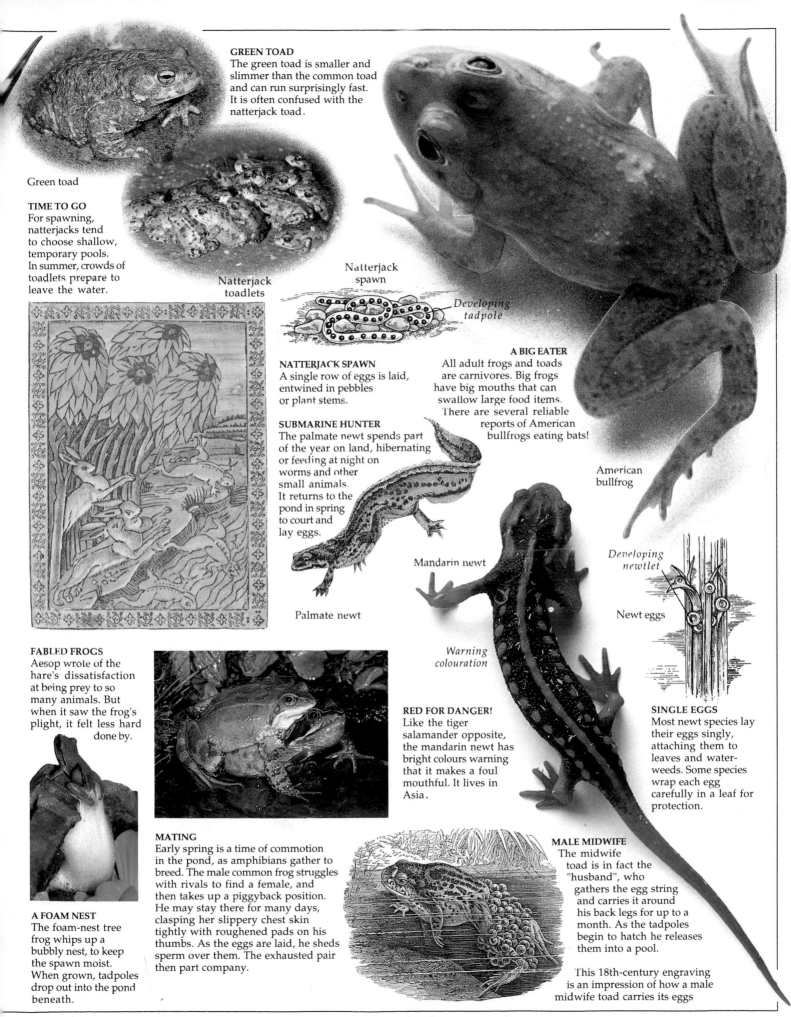

GREEN TOAD
The green toad is smaller and slimmer than the common toad and can run surprisingly fast. It is often confused with the natterjack toad.

Green toad

TIME TO GO
For spawning, natterjacks tend to choose shallow, temporary pools. In summer, crowds of toadlets prepare to leave the water.

Natterjack toadlets

Natterjack spawn

Developing tadpole

NATTERJACK SPAWN
A single row of eggs is laid, entwined in pebbles or plant stems.

SUBMARINE HUNTER
The palmate newt spends part of the year on land, hibernating or feeding at night on worms and other small animals. It returns to the pond in spring to court and lay eggs.

Mandarin newt

Palmate newt

A BIG EATER
All adult frogs and toads are carnivores. Big frogs have big mouths that can swallow large food items. There are several reliable reports of American bullfrogs eating bats!

American bullfrog

Developing newtlet

Newt eggs

FABLED FROGS
Aesop wrote of the hare's dissatisfaction at being prey to so many animals. But when it saw the frog's plight, it felt less hard done by.

Warning colouration

RED FOR DANGER!
Like the tiger salamander opposite, the mandarin newt has bright colours warning that it makes a foul mouthful. It lives in Asia.

SINGLE EGGS
Most newt species lay their eggs singly, attaching them to leaves and water-weeds. Some species wrap each egg carefully in a leaf for protection.

A FOAM NEST
The foam-nest tree frog whips up a bubbly nest, to keep the spawn moist. When grown, tadpoles drop out into the pond beneath.

MATING
Early spring is a time of commotion in the pond, as amphibians gather to breed. The male common frog struggles with rivals to find a female, and then takes up a piggyback position. He may stay there for many days, clasping her slippery chest skin tightly with roughened pads on his thumbs. As the eggs are laid, he sheds sperm over them. The exhausted pair then part company.

MALE MIDWIFE
The midwife toad is in fact the "husband", who gathers the egg string and carries it around his back legs for up to a month. As the tadpoles begin to hatch he releases them into a pool.

This 18th-century engraving is an impression of how a male midwife toad carries its eggs

39

Hunters in the water

MORE THAN 300 MILLION YEARS AGO, the reptiles appeared on Earth. They probably evolved from amphibians (pp. 38-9). Their big advantage was that they had made a complete break from an aquatic environment. Unlike amphibians, which needed water in which to lay their jelly-covered eggs, reptiles had hard-shelled eggs that could be laid on land. Soon, as dinosaurs, they would come to dominate life on land. Since that time, however, some groups of reptiles have made an "evolutionary U-turn" and gone back to life in the water. Many snakes readily take to water, swim well, and hunt fish, frogs, aquatic insects and land creatures that come to the pond or riverside for a drink. Indeed, certain groups of reptiles, such as crocodiles and turtles, have never really left the aquatic environment, though they come on to land to lay their eggs.

GIANT IN THE WATER
One of the longest, and certainly the heaviest, of snakes is the water boa, or anaconda, of northern South America. Lengths of 9 m (30 ft) and weights of over 200 kg (440 lb) have been recorded. It can consume creatures as large as a pig.

Water moccasin

DOWN IN THE SWAMPS
This old engraving shows the water moccasin, a venomous swamp dweller of the south eastern USA. When this snake is threatened it opens its mouth wide to reveal the white inside lining, hence its other name of "cottonmouth".

Viperine water snake

Zig-zag markings on the snake's back are similar to those of a common viper, or adder

Snake swims by undulations of its body

Turtle...or terrapin?

There is little biological distinction between a turtle and a terrapin. Most experts call the entire group (chelonians) turtles. Small, freshwater species may be named terrapins, from a North American Indian word that referred originally to the diamondback terrapin. But the numerous exceptions confuse the issue. Whatever our labels, however, many turtles are well equipped for an aquatic life, either in fresh water or in the sea. Some have webbed or flipper-like feet, and leathery skin overlying the shell on their underside, through which oxygen can be absorbed. They tend to be omnivores, taking aquatic animals, fruit from bankside trees, and carrion as they become available.

SCARCELY A RIPPLE
The viperine water snake of Europe is quite at home in the water, swimming easily across its surface. It will strike at virtually any suitably sized prey, from fish to frogs and even small mammals. Adults grow to 80 cm (2.5 ft) or more (this one is approximately life-sized, but young). Despite its name and its zig-zag markings reminiscent of the adder, it is not poisonous, being a relative of the grass snake.

Yellow-bellied terrapin

Distinctive brown and yellow markings

OPPOSITE FEET FORWARD
The yellow-bellied terrapin may walk along the bed of a river or lake, or swim by paddling alternately with two limbs - the front foot on one side and the back foot on the other.

Left-hand foreleg is forward when right-hand foreleg is back

Smooth plates on shell

Shell lacks bony plates

Ridged bony plates on shell

Strong horny jaws in mouth

Soft-shelled turtle

Webbed feet for swimming

THE SOFT SHELL
Soft-shelled turtles lack the hard, bony plates carried by the hard-shelled types. This life-size youngster will grow to about 30 cm (1 ft) long.

SNAPPY CUSTOMER
This young common snapper will reach almost 50 cm (20 in) when adult. Its strong, sharp-ridged jaws will be able to crack the shells of other turtles which form part of its diet.

Common snapper

Water snakes will eat all kinds of freshwater life, including this unfortunate frog

DIVING DRAGON
Eastern water dragons frequent watercourses in eastern Australia. This lizard is a powerful swimmer, using its vertically flattened tail and long legs. It has a body length of nearly 1 m (3 ft), a tail more than double this, and it eats all manner of water and shore life, from worms and frogs to shellfish, small mammals and fruit.

Eastern water dragon

41

Floating flowers

IN ANCIENT TIMES people were amazed to see that, when a previously dry watercourse filled with recent rains, the splendid blooms of water-lilies would soon appear.

Flowerbud

These aquatic plants gained a reputation as a symbol of immortality; the ancient Egyptians even worshipped one type of water-lily, the sacred lotus. Water-lily flowers are made more mysterious by their daily routine: they remain closed during the morning, open to reveal their beauty at around noon, and towards evening close again and perhaps sink slightly into the water. On overcast days they might not open fully at all. This may be an adaptation to aid pollination by flying insects, which are more likely to be active in the afternoon's warmth. During dull weather, signifying wind and rain, the closed flowers are less likely to be swamped. The flowers and leaves grow on tough, rubbery stems - 3 m (10 ft) long in some species - anchored in the mud on the beds of ponds, lakes and slow rivers.

THE "BEAUTIFUL NUISANCE"
The water hyacinth is a free-floating flowering plant which spreads rapidly, often clogging rivers, canals and ditches.

Red hybrid - "Escarboucle"

Leaves may be heart-shaped, oval or round

Yellow water-lily leaves are patterned with a red tinge

White water-lily flower

Leathery leaves repel water droplets

Pink hybrid

Conspicuous yellow stamens

LILIES AND THEIR HYBRIDS
There are some 60 species of water-lily around
the world (in some areas they are known as lotuses).
Their beautiful waxy-looking flowers and bold
circular leaves have made them favourites in ponds,
ornamental water gardens and landscaped lakes.
Horticulturalists have bred many differently
coloured flowers.

Yellow hybrid
"Chromatella"

Waxy petals

Pink hybrid

FLOATING SAUCERS
Some of the largest leaves of any plant
belong to the Amazonian water lily.
A single leaf may be more than 1.5 m (5 ft)
across, with an upturned rim and stiff
reinforcing ribs beneath.

LILY LEAF CASE
The china mark moth's caterpillar cuts out
an oval of leaf, fastening it to the underside
with silk thread
to form a
protective
case.

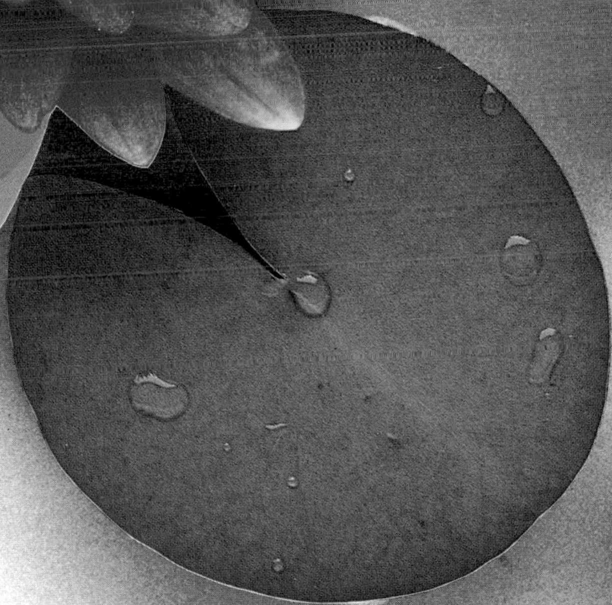

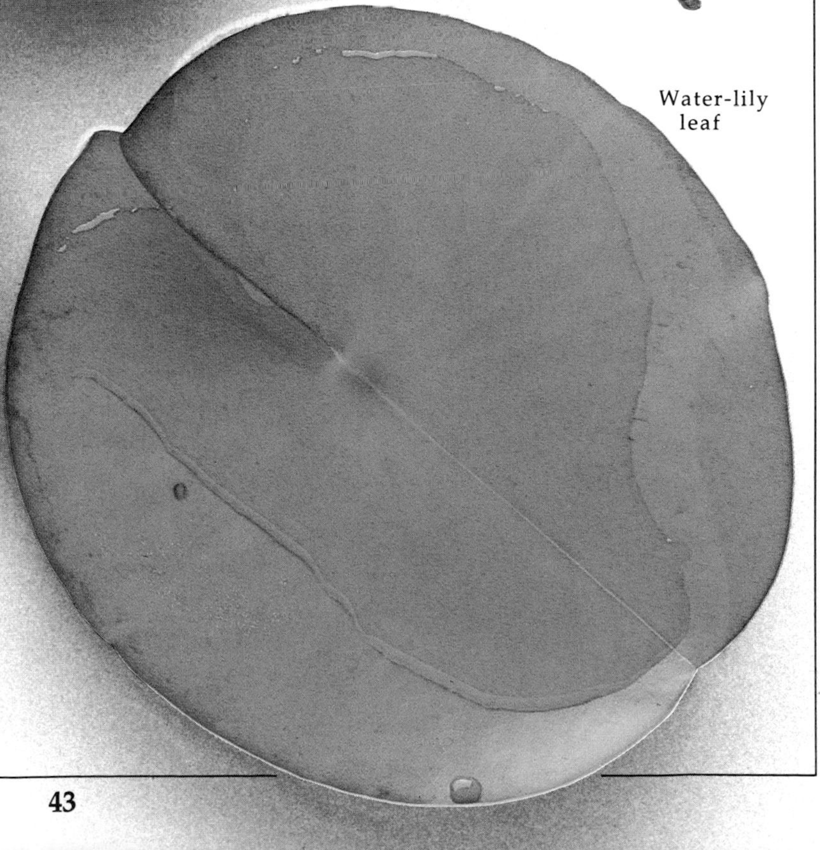

Water-lily
leaf

WELL-USED LEAVES
The leaves (lily "pads") are used by many water creatures.
Pond snails browse on them and lay their speckled, jelly-sausage
egg masses (p. 8) on their undersides. Frogs rest on or under them,
waiting to snap up unwary insects. In some places the pads grow so
densely that certain creatures can walk on them. A bird, the African
jacana, has long, widespread toes and is known as the "lily trotter",
as it steps delicately on the leaves in its search for insects and seeds.

Plants at the pond's surface

MANY WATER PLANTS are not rooted in the mud at the bottom of the pond, but are free to float over the surface of the water. Most have trailing roots that balance the plant and absorb minerals, although some have no roots at all. At first sight, these plants seem to have few problems. Unlike some land plants, they are well supported and, out in the middle of the pond, they cannot be shaded by trees or taller plants. But there are disadvantages: the water's surface can be whipped by the wind into waves that drag and tear at them; rain might collect on a leaf and sink it, or the leaf may be frozen underwater!

SMALLEST PLANTS
The duckweeds are among the smallest and simplest flowering plants in the world. Flowers are only produced in shallow water that receives plenty of sunlight. The "leaves" contain air-filled spaces called lacunae that keep them afloat.

Tiny roots absorb minerals from the water

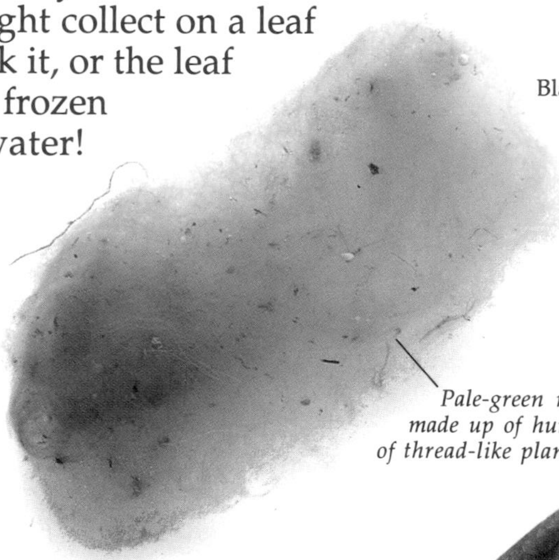

Blanket weed

Surface view

Side view

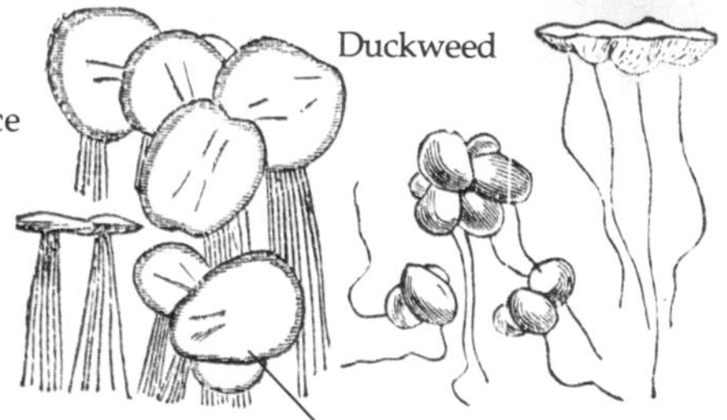

Duckweed

Three of the many species of duckweed are shown here

Pale-green mass is made up of hundreds of thread-like plants

New plants produced by side-shoots that break off and float away

A GREEN BLANKET
"Blanket weed" is a popular name for the green hair-like masses of algae that burst into growth in the spring. These plants can spread so quickly that they cover the surface like a blanket of green cotton-wool, blocking out light to the plants below.

Two new leaves developing from old leaf

Ivy-leaved duckweed

FLOWERING FLOATER
This engraving shows another species of duckweed that floats on the water surface only when it is flowering, otherwise it floats just under the water surface. The ivy-leaf shape is formed when two new leaves develop, one on each side of the original leaf.

Water-lily leaf and flowerbud (pp. 42-3)

CIRCLE OF STRENGTH
Like many other floating leaves, those of water-lilies have a rounded outline. This design probably helps to prevent tearing, when wind ruffles the pond surface. The shiny upper surface repels rainwater so that the leaves are not swamped by a shower. Lilies are not true floating plants because they are rooted in the mud (pp. 42-3).

Azolla water fern

Pink tinge develops to deep red in autumn

Thread-like roots trail beneath the plant

Leaves are similar in shape to water-lily leaves

WINTER SEEDS AND BUDS
Frogbit, a relative of water soldier (below), has a similar technique for avoiding the ice and frost of winter. In this case, however, the parts that overwinter are the seeds and the specially grown, dense "winter buds". Both are produced in the autumn and sink to rest in the mud, until the increasing light levels and temperatures of spring spur them into growth, when they float to the surface again. In summer, the delicate white flowers and kidney-shaped leaves carpet whole ponds and ditches.

FLOATING FRONDS
Azolla is not a flowering plant but a fern, so technically its delicately sculptured "leaves" are called fronds. Tiny hairs repel water and prevent the fronds becoming waterlogged and sinking.

Frogbit

Trailing roots

Plants will sometimes root in shallow water

Water soldier

GREEN ROSETTES
The rosettes of water soldier spend summer floating at or near the pond surface. As autumn approaches, the leaves develop a limy coating that weighs them down. The plant sinks, to avoid winter's frost and ice. Fresh spring leaves buoy it up again. This plant reproduces by sending out runners that root at a distance, and by male and female flowers borne on separate plants.

WATER SOLDIER IN FLOWER
White flowers are produced in midsummer, male and female flowers on different plants. Once flowering is over, the plant sinks to the bottom of the pond.

Long, unbranched roots hang down under the plant to balance it

45

Underwater weeds

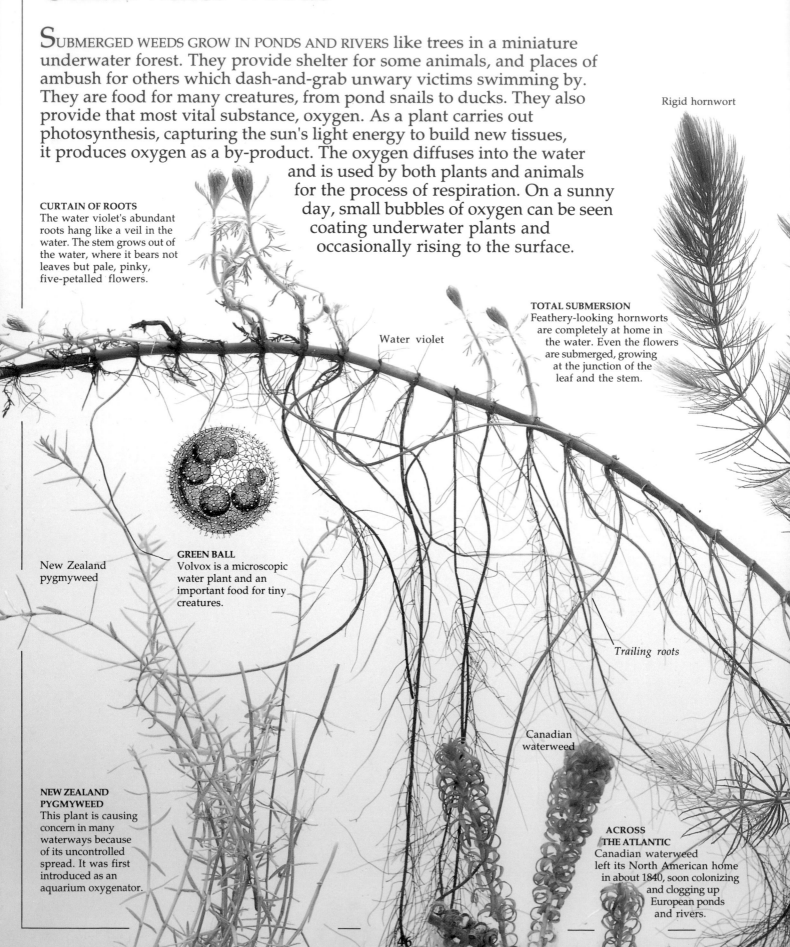

Sᴜʙᴍᴇʀɢᴇᴅ ᴡᴇᴇᴅs ɢʀᴏᴡ ɪɴ ᴘᴏɴᴅs ᴀɴᴅ ʀɪᴠᴇʀs like trees in a miniature underwater forest. They provide shelter for some animals, and places of ambush for others which dash-and-grab unwary victims swimming by. They are food for many creatures, from pond snails to ducks. They also provide that most vital substance, oxygen. As a plant carries out photosynthesis, capturing the sun's light energy to build new tissues, it produces oxygen as a by-product. The oxygen diffuses into the water and is used by both plants and animals for the process of respiration. On a sunny day, small bubbles of oxygen can be seen coating underwater plants and occasionally rising to the surface.

Rigid hornwort

CURTAIN OF ROOTS
The water violet's abundant roots hang like a veil in the water. The stem grows out of the water, where it bears not leaves but pale, pinky, five-petalled flowers.

TOTAL SUBMERSION
Feathery-looking hornworts are completely at home in the water. Even the flowers are submerged, growing at the junction of the leaf and the stem.

Water violet

New Zealand pygmyweed

GREEN BALL
Volvox is a microscopic water plant and an important food for tiny creatures.

Trailing roots

NEW ZEALAND PYGMYWEED
This plant is causing concern in many waterways because of its uncontrolled spread. It was first introduced as an aquarium oxygenator.

Canadian waterweed

ACROSS THE ATLANTIC
Canadian waterweed left its North American home in about 1840, soon colonizing and clogging up European ponds and rivers.

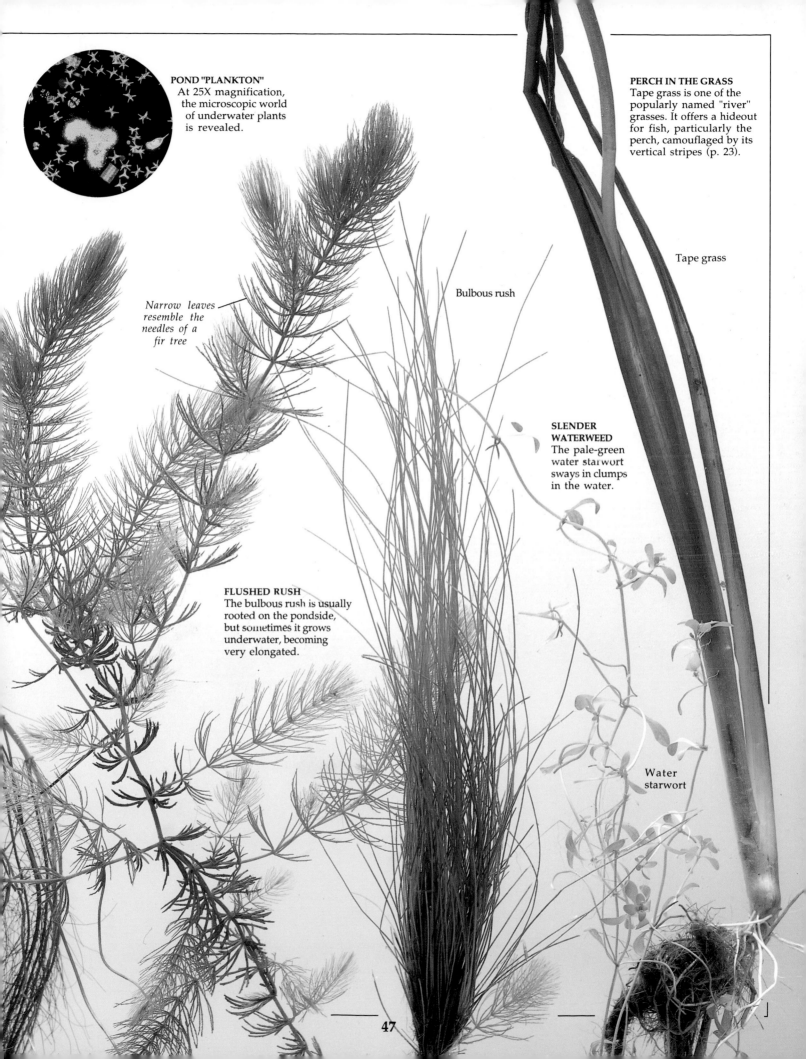

POND "PLANKTON"
At 25X magnification, the microscopic world of underwater plants is revealed.

PERCH IN THE GRASS
Tape grass is one of the popularly named "river" grasses. It offers a hideout for fish, particularly the perch, camouflaged by its vertical stripes (p. 23).

Tape grass

Narrow leaves resemble the needles of a fir tree

Bulbous rush

SLENDER WATERWEED
The pale-green water starwort sways in clumps in the water.

FLUSHED RUSH
The bulbous rush is usually rooted on the pondside, but sometimes it grows underwater, becoming very elongated.

Water starwort

Dragonflies and damselflies

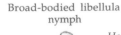

THESE LARGE, POWERFUL FLIERS speed to and fro along the bank and over the water's surface, searching out their food of small airborne creatures with their enormous eyes. Like those of other insects, the dragonfly's eyes are made up of many separate lenses that probably give a mosaic-like picture of the world. As the adults dart about above, the water-dwelling nymphs crawl on the pond bottom. Like their parents, they seize and eat any small creature they can catch, from other water insects to tadpoles and fish.

Damselflies

These are smaller and more slender relatives of dragonflies. Although at first glance they appear very similar in shape and lifestyle, there are several important differences that distinguish them from the dragonflies - most obviously the fact that the damselfly holds its two pairs of wings together over its back when resting, while the dragonfly holds them out flat at the sides of its body.

SIMILAR WINGS
A damselfly's wings are roughly equal in size, with rounded ends, unlike the dragonfly's wings.

Emerald damselfly

Eyes protrude from side of head

Rounded wing tips

Blue-tailed damselfly

MALE AND FEMALE
In most damselflies, the female has a slightly wider and less colourful abdomen than the male.

Azure damselfly

Large red damselfly

WEAK FLIERS
Damselflies tend to be weaker fliers than their dragonfly cousins.

SMALLER EYES
The small eyes of the damselfly are set on the sides of the head, while dragonflies' eyes meet at the top of the head.

Cast nymphal skin

Broad-bodied libellula nymph

Young southern hawker nymph

Mask — *Hooks on mask impale prey* — *Mask*

THE DEADLY MASK
Dragonfly nymphs are the scourge of the pond, eating anything they can catch with their "mask". This is a horny flap, equivalent to the lower lip, which has two vicious hooks at the end (above). Normally the mask is folded under the head, but it is hinged so that it can suddenly shoot out to impale prey, which is then pulled back to the mouth.

CAST-OFF CLOTHING
This perfectly detailed empty skin is from a brown hawker dragonfly's final moult. New adults usually emerge at night or early in the morning, to avoid predators.

THE MATING GAME
The male dragonfly clasps the female and she bends to pick up the sperm from a special organ at the front of his abdomen.

THE LIFE OF THE DRAGONFLY
A dragonfly begins life as an egg laid in water. It hatches into a larva that grows by splitting its skin and forming a new, larger skin. There are between eight and 15 moults over two years or more, depending on the species. A gradual change to adult form like this (compared with a sudden change, for example caterpillar to butterfly) is called "incomplete metamorphosis", and the intermediate larval stages are referred to as "nymphs". Finally the nymph climbs up a stem into the air, splits its skin a final time, and the adult emerges.

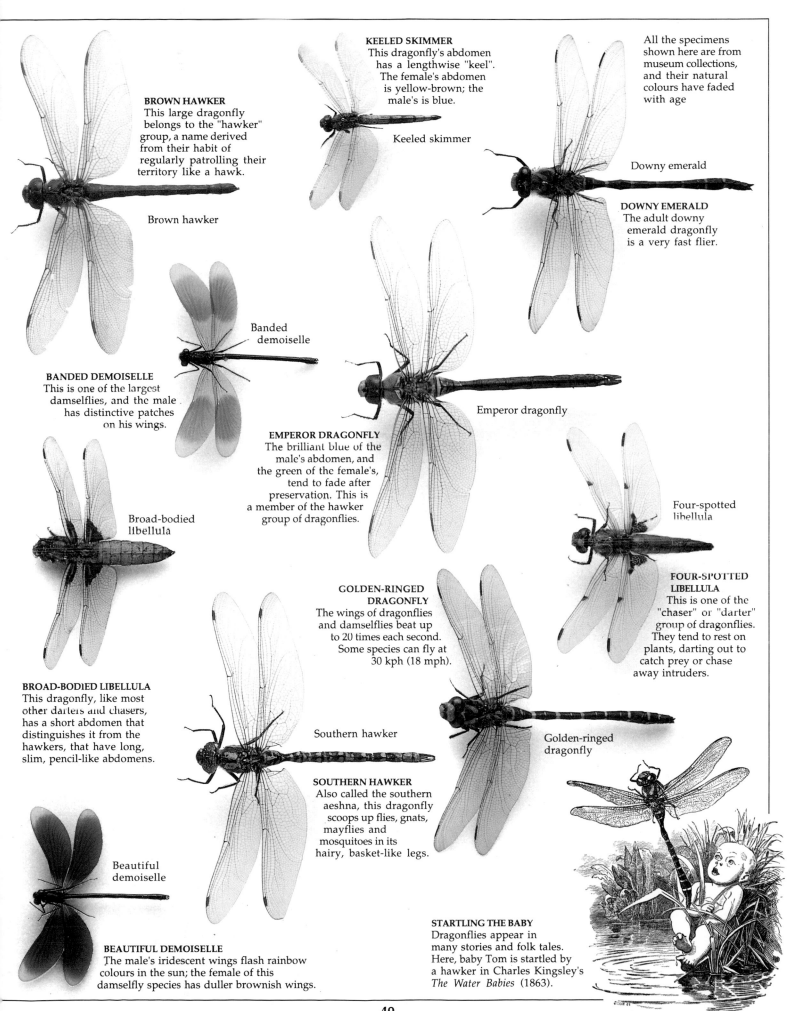

BROWN HAWKER
This large dragonfly belongs to the "hawker" group, a name derived from their habit of regularly patrolling their territory like a hawk.

Brown hawker

KEELED SKIMMER
This dragonfly's abdomen has a lengthwise "keel". The female's abdomen is yellow-brown; the male's is blue.

Keeled skimmer

All the specimens shown here are from museum collections, and their natural colours have faded with age

Downy emerald

DOWNY EMERALD
The adult downy emerald dragonfly is a very fast flier.

Banded demoiselle

BANDED DEMOISELLE
This is one of the largest damselflies, and the male has distinctive patches on his wings.

Broad-bodied libellula

EMPEROR DRAGONFLY
The brilliant blue of the male's abdomen, and the green of the female's, tend to fade after preservation. This is a member of the hawker group of dragonflies.

Emperor dragonfly

Four-spotted libellula

FOUR-SPOTTED LIBELLULA
This is one of the "chaser" or "darter" group of dragonflies. They tend to rest on plants, darting out to catch prey or chase away intruders.

GOLDEN-RINGED DRAGONFLY
The wings of dragonflies and damselflies beat up to 20 times each second. Some species can fly at 30 kph (18 mph).

BROAD-BODIED LIBELLULA
This dragonfly, like most other darters and chasers, has a short abdomen that distinguishes it from the hawkers, that have long, slim, pencil-like abdomens.

Southern hawker

Golden-ringed dragonfly

SOUTHERN HAWKER
Also called the southern aeshna, this dragonfly scoops up flies, gnats, mayflies and mosquitoes in its hairy, basket-like legs.

Beautiful demoiselle

BEAUTIFUL DEMOISELLE
The male's iridescent wings flash rainbow colours in the sun; the female of this damselfly species has duller brownish wings.

STARTLING THE BABY
Dragonflies appear in many stories and folk tales. Here, baby Tom is startled by a hawker in Charles Kingsley's *The Water Babies* (1863).

Insects in the water

Insects, the most adaptable creatures on earth, can live in places ranging from glaciers to hot springs, and deserts to tropical forests. About half of the 25 major groups of insects live in fresh water. Some, such as water beetles and bugs, spend nearly all their lives in water. Others, like mayflies and caddis flies, have a watery "childhood" and emerge into the air when adult. Certain aquatic insects, including the water beetles, are air-breathing and visit the surface regularly to obtain supplies, which they store by various ingenious means (p. 51). Others have specialized "gills" to extract oxygen from the water, while still others can absorb sufficient dissolved oxygen through their skin.

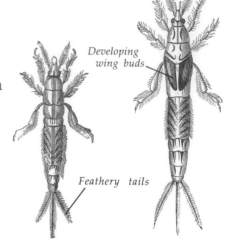

Developing wing buds

Feathery tails

Like dragonfly larvae (p. 48), mayfly larvae are called nymphs

As the nymph matures, small "wing buds" grow with each moult

Rat-tailed maggots (drone fly larvae)

Adult drone fly

Adult mayfly

MAGGOT'S PARENT
The rat-tailed maggot is the larva of the drone fly, a type of hoverfly, named for its resemblance to the drones of the honey bee.

Breathing tube

Long "tails" identify this insect

MAGGOT WITH SNORKEL *above*
The rat-tailed maggot has a long breathing tube of three sections that telescope into one another. It lives in the mud of shallow ponds, sucking up decaying food.

STICKS AND STONES
Many species of caddis fly have aquatic larvae that build protective cases around themselves. The construction material is characteristic of each species. As the larva grows, it adds more material to the front of the case.

THREE-TAILED FLY
Like its larvae, the adult mayfly has three very distinctive trailing "tails". Mayflies are known as "spinners" by anglers.

GROWN-UP CADDIS
Adult caddis flies are less well-known than their water-dwelling youngsters. The adults are drab grey or brown, come out at dusk or night, and are easily confused with small moths. They flit about near water, rarely feed, and seldom live more than a few days.

Larval cases may be attached to water plants or lie on the pond bottom

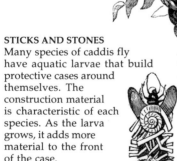

Case is extended by adding material to the front end

Head of larva emerges from case to feed

Every species makes a distinctive case

SPRING FEAST
Mayfly adults emerge in huge swarms in spring. They fly weakly, have no mouths and so cannot feed, and spend their few days of adult life mating and laying eggs by dipping their abdomens in water. The "dance of the mayflies" attracts hungry fish - and anglers, who use mayfly lures to catch trout.

Adult caddis flies

Wings covered with fine hairs

Antennae often as long as the body

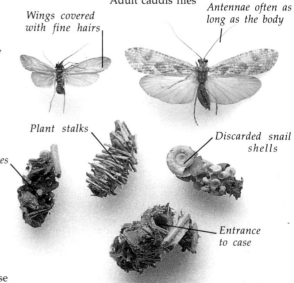

Plant stalks

Small stones

Discarded snail shells

Entrance to case

Cases built by caddis-fly larvae

*Front legs
seize prey* Water stick insect

*Front legs catch
tadpoles and
other prey*

Pond skater

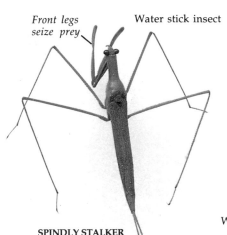

Water
scorpion

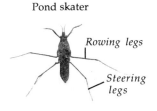

Rowing legs

*Steering
legs*

DEAD LEAF?
When disturbed, the
water scorpion sinks to
the bottom and stays
still, looking like a dead
leaf. This is a smaller
species.

WATER-WALKER
The back four feet of the
pond skater have thick pads
of hair that repel water,
so preventing this bug from
sinking as it rows across
the surface of the pond.

Water scorpion

SPINDLY STALKER
The water stick insect
grabs any small underwater
creature with its mantis-like
front legs, and then sucks the
juices from inside, using its
needle-shaped mouthparts.
A short trip to the surface
allows fresh supplies of air to
be sucked through the long
tail, the two parts of which
are usually held together
by bristles to form a tube.

*Breathing
tube*

Wing covers

Water boatman

*Hair-covered
legs for
swimming*

Backswimmer

WATER BOATMAN
This insect's name refers to
the oar-like rowing motions
of its legs as it propels itself
through the water. It eats
any plant debris or algae it
can grub up or catch in its
sieve-like front legs.

*Parts of
breathing tube*

STING IN THE TAIL?
No, the "tail" of the water
scorpion is a harmless
breathing tube, unlike the
poisonous version of its
dry-land namesake. The
dangerous parts are the
powerful claw-like front
legs and stinging beak-
shaped mouth.

BACKSWIMMER . . .
A bug not a beetle, this
unusual top view of a
backswimmer shows its
hard wing cases that cover
strong flying wings. Most
of its time, however, is
spent hanging upside-down
below the water surface.

Air bubble

THE BUBBLE CHAMBER
The air-breathing water
spider (not actually an
insect, but an arachnid),
makes a "diving bell"
to live in. It weaves a
web among water plants
and stocks it with air
from the surface (below).
The air being transported
in its body hairs gives
the spider's abdomen
a silvery sheen (left).

BEETLE POWER
In a small pond, the great diving beetle has few
predators, but many prey - insects, tadpoles and
small fish such as this unlucky stickleback.

SPARE AIR
Water beetles are air-breathing
insects and have devised clever
methods for collecting air from
the surface. Many aquatic beetles
trap air on the hairs under the
body. Others trap air under their
wing cases, making them buoyant
and always struggling to swim
downwards. Some, like the silver
water beetle shown here, use
both methods.

Silver water beetle

Freshwater shells

ALL THE LIFE-SIZED SHELLS shown here have two features in common: their builder-owners live in fresh water, and they belong to the mollusc group. The mollusc's shell is made chiefly of calcium-containing minerals such as calcium carbonate (lime). To make its shell, the animal must absorb minerals from the water. In general, aquatic molluscs are more common in hard-water areas, where water is naturally richer in dissolved minerals. The snails and limpets (gastropods) are mostly grazers, on water plants and the algal "scum" on submerged stones, although some species can filter-feed. The mussels and cockles (bivalves) feed by sucking in a stream of water and filtering out tiny food particles.

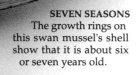

SEVEN SEASONS
The growth rings on this swan mussel's shell show that it is about six or seven years old.

How do molluscs breathe?

Water snails are divided into two groups, depending on how they breathe. The great pond snail, ramshorn snail and bladder snail are known as pulmonates - they breathe air, like land snails. They float up to the surface, open a breathing aperture and take a gulp of air into a lung-like cavity. The other group, including valve, river and spire snails, are called prosobranchs. They breathe by absorbing oxygen from the water through gills.

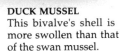

DUCK MUSSEL
This bivalve's shell is more swollen than that of the swan mussel.

RIGHT-HANDERS
Usually great pond snail shells curl to the right, but "left-handers" are known.

SEE-THROUGH SNAIL
The nautilus ramshorn is so small that its shell is semi-transparent.

BIVALVE LARDER
Pea mussels are the staple food of many fish and water birds.

WANDERING SNAIL
The whorls of this wandering snail are compressed at its tip.

CURLY WHORLY
The tightly coiled white ramshorn is from ponds and streams.

MARBLED SNAIL
The nerite snail has an attractively stippled and whorled shell.

JOINTED SHELL
The horny pea cockle is a bivalve mollusc as it has two shells.

River shellfish

The molluscs below and left (swan and duck mussels) tend to frequent flowing water, compared to the still waters of ponds and lakes. The growth rings of the mussels indicate their age, which might be up to a dozen years for a large individual. Growth rings can be seen on snails too, but they are less clearly divided into a year-by-year pattern.

Snails grow by adding new material at the open end of the shell

TWISTING TUBE
Snail shells are coiled, gradually widening tubes, clearly seen on this Lister's river snail.

MINERAL COLLECTOR
River snail's shells may be over 5 cm (2 in) long - a lot of calcium to collect.

LISTENING SNAIL
The ear pond snail's flared opening resembles a human ear.

SWOLLEN JOINT
This tumid unio mussel has an inflated "umbo" near its hinge-line.

ZEBRA MUSSEL
This bivalve is anchored to rocks by sticky byssus threads.

WATERWEED EATER
The great ramshorn water snail browses on underwater plants.

DISTINCTIVE SHELL
The last whorl on the bladder snail's shell is very large.

STUBBY AND SHINY
These shiny, compact shells belong to the common bithynia.

BITHYNIA LEACHI
These bithynias have no common name; only a scientific name.

STRAIGHT SNAIL
The river limpet is a true snail, but its shell is not coiled.

OPEN AND SHUT
The "valve" of the valve snail is the door or operculum, of its shell.

SLOW WATER
The lake limpet can often be found in slow-flowing rivers.

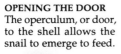

OPENING THE DOOR
The operculum, or door, to the shell allows the snail to emerge to feed.

Operculum makes a watertight seal to shell when closed

TWO TINY SHELLS
Pea cockles are tiny, filter-feeding bivalve molluscs.

SALTY AND FRESH
Jenkin's spire shells are found in estuaries as well as in ponds and rivers.

Head of the river

MANY RIVERS begin life as fast-flowing upland streams, cascading across moors or through craggy woodlands. The deep, rocky gulleys, the overhanging trees and the splashing waters create contrasting worlds: shady, damp banks with lush green vegetation, and streambeds where rushing water washes away nearly all plant life and any but the most tenaciously clinging animals. In a flood, entire plant and animal communities may be swept away. Yet new seeds and spores soon spring up, while creatures creep out from under rocks to fight their way back upstream.

Dipper

UNDERWATER WALKER
The dipper bobs its head as it stands on midstream rocks, watching for small animal prey. It can also walk along the river bed, head facing upstream and tail acting as a hydroplane in the current, to keep its feet firmly on the bottom.

ARMOURED CRAYFISH
Hard water is favoured by the freshwater crayfish, a relative of the marine lobster. It needs plenty of calcium minerals to build its shell.

Hard outer shell made up from minerals in the water

Freshwater crayfish

BANKSIDE MOISTURE-LOVERS
Succulent growths of mosses, liverworts, ferns and other damp-loving plants colonize the banks and splash-zone rocks. The larger heart-shaped leaves are marsh violet.

Polytrichum moss

Fern

Puffball

Liverwort

YOUNG BALL
Fungi, such as this young member of the puffball group, relish shady streamside conditions.

Great woodrush

Liverwort

LICHEN BRANCH
Shady, damp conditions are ideal for certain lichens, which are co-operative combinations of fungi and algae. Two different kinds of leafy lichen are growing on this branch.

Marsh violet

Bullhead

UPSTREAM FISH
Despite the fast current fish, such as the bullhead, are found at the head of the river. The bullhead's flattened shape allows it to hide under stones.

Oak leaves

FOOD FROM ABOVE
Trees such as the oak hang over the water, and their fruits and leaves provide sustenance for river-dwellers if they fall into the water.

Fontinalis moss

Acorns

Galls caused by insects living in oak leaves

Deeply divided fronds

Great woodrush

UNDERWATER MOSS
Fontinalis or "willow moss" undulates with the current in slower streams and rivers, anchored to a stone or fallen log.

Shiny, undivided fronds

BETWEEN THE BOULDERS
Groups of midstream boulders often support a thriving island of life; here, great woodrush sprouts from current-collected soil.

Rows of spores

Layer of moss growing on boulders

Male fern

FEATHERY FRONDS
Many types of ferns thrive in the shaded, humid conditions along riverbanks. The hart's-tongue fern (far right) has rib-like rows of brown spore cases on the undersides of its fronds. It is unusual among ferns in having solid, unbranched fronds.

Feathery, pale-green fronds

Shiny, dark-green fronds

Hard fern

Lady fern

Hart's-tongue fern

Brown spore cases

55

Life along the riverbank

As STREAMS BECOME MORE SEDATE, and their courses join up and widen, the river comes into being. But when does a stream become a river? One definition is that streams are less than 5 m (15 ft) wide, while rivers are more. Larger rivers usually have a slower current, allowing rooted plants to flourish at the water's edge. Whatever the distinction, riverbank life suits many kinds of plants and animals. On a high-banked river, the soil at the water's edge is nearly always saturated, but it becomes drier higher up the bank. So there is often a characteristic zonation of plant life, with mud-rooted irises and water plantains lower down, and the damp-ground hemp agrimony, balsam and similar flowers slightly higher.

Thistle-shaped flowerhead

Messing about on the river has long been a favourite leisure pursuit

FIVE IN ONE
Each small "flower" of hemp agrimony is a cluster of five even smaller "florets".

ABOUT TO FLOWER
This teasel's flower is just emerging, its pinkish-mauve petals not yet visible.

Hooks attach fruits to passing animals

Teasel

Spiny flowerhead is still developing

Heart-shaped leaves are slightly downy

Explosive seed cases are developing inside the flowers

Leaves have toothed edges

Hemp agrimony

HITCHING A RIDE
Young great burdock flowers already bear the hooks that, when the seeds ripen, will catch on fur, coats and socks.

TRAVELLING FLOWER
Indian, or Himalayan, balsam, a native of that region, is a greenhouse escapee. It has spread along many riverbanks, ditch sides and damp gulleys.

Leaves have serrated margins

Stem has reddish tinge

Indian balsam
(Himalayan balsam)

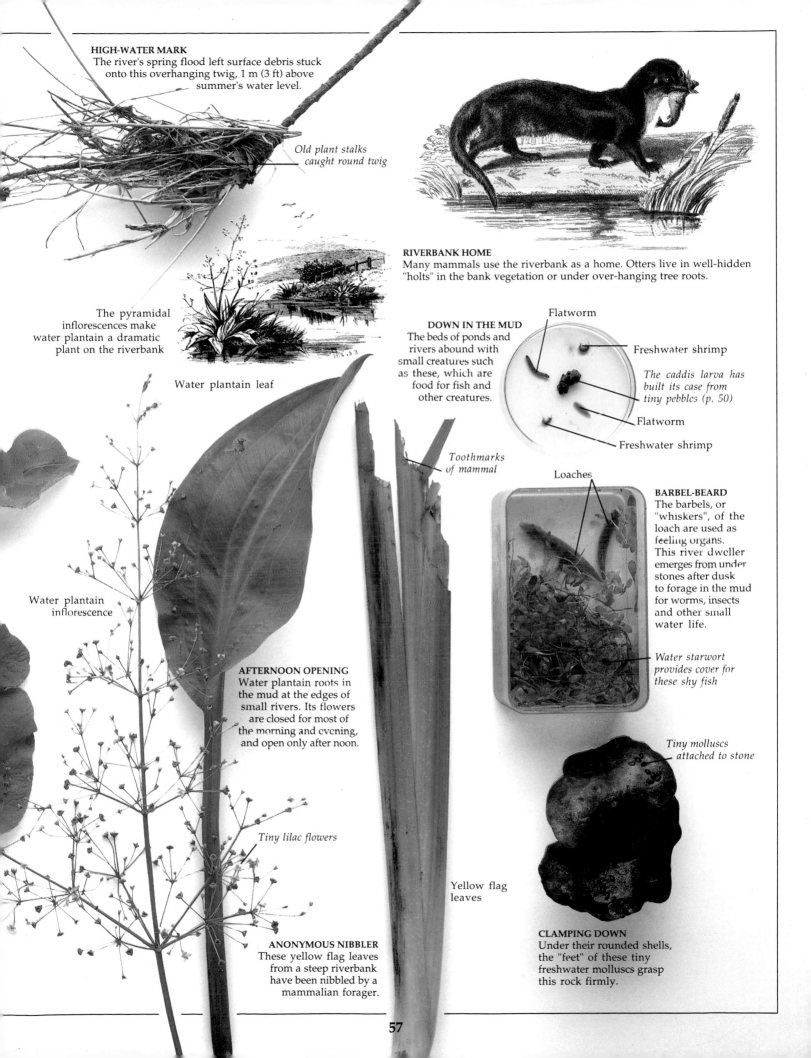

HIGH-WATER MARK
The river's spring flood left surface debris stuck onto this overhanging twig, 1 m (3 ft) above summer's water level.

Old plant stalks caught round twig

The pyramidal inflorescences make water plantain a dramatic plant on the riverbank

Water plantain leaf

Water plantain inflorescence

RIVERBANK HOME
Many mammals use the riverbank as a home. Otters live in well-hidden "holts" in the bank vegetation or under over-hanging tree roots.

Flatworm

DOWN IN THE MUD
The beds of ponds and rivers abound with small creatures such as these, which are food for fish and other creatures.

Freshwater shrimp

The caddis larva has built its case from tiny pebbles (p. 50)

Flatworm

Freshwater shrimp

Toothmarks of mammal

Loaches

BARBEL-BEARD
The barbels, or "whiskers", of the loach are used as feeling organs. This river dweller emerges from under stones after dusk to forage in the mud for worms, insects and other small water life.

Water starwort provides cover for these shy fish

AFTERNOON OPENING
Water plantain roots in the mud at the edges of small rivers. Its flowers are closed for most of the morning and evening, and open only after noon.

Tiny lilac flowers

Tiny molluscs attached to stone

Yellow flag leaves

ANONYMOUS NIBBLER
These yellow flag leaves from a steep riverbank have been nibbled by a mammalian forager.

CLAMPING DOWN
Under their rounded shells, the "feet" of these tiny freshwater molluscs grasp this rock firmly.

The river's mouth

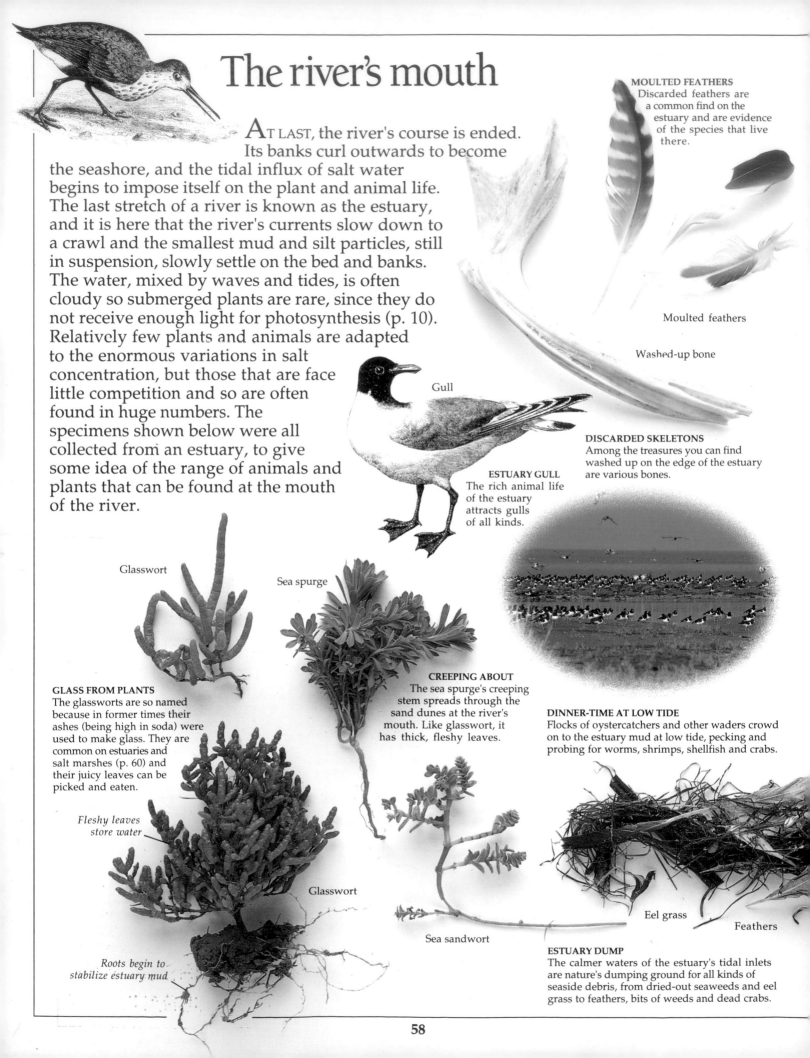

A<small>T LAST</small>, the river's course is ended. Its banks curl outwards to become the seashore, and the tidal influx of salt water begins to impose itself on the plant and animal life. The last stretch of a river is known as the estuary, and it is here that the river's currents slow down to a crawl and the smallest mud and silt particles, still in suspension, slowly settle on the bed and banks. The water, mixed by waves and tides, is often cloudy so submerged plants are rare, since they do not receive enough light for photosynthesis (p. 10). Relatively few plants and animals are adapted to the enormous variations in salt concentration, but those that are face little competition and so are often found in huge numbers. The specimens shown below were all collected from an estuary, to give some idea of the range of animals and plants that can be found at the mouth of the river.

MOULTED FEATHERS
Discarded feathers are a common find on the estuary and are evidence of the species that live there.

Moulted feathers

Washed-up bone

Gull

ESTUARY GULL
The rich animal life of the estuary attracts gulls of all kinds.

DISCARDED SKELETONS
Among the treasures you can find washed up on the edge of the estuary are various bones.

Glasswort

Sea spurge

GLASS FROM PLANTS
The glassworts are so named because in former times their ashes (being high in soda) were used to make glass. They are common on estuaries and salt marshes (p. 60) and their juicy leaves can be picked and eaten.

Fleshy leaves store water

CREEPING ABOUT
The sea spurge's creeping stem spreads through the sand dunes at the river's mouth. Like glasswort, it has thick, fleshy leaves.

DINNER-TIME AT LOW TIDE
Flocks of oystercatchers and other waders crowd on to the estuary mud at low tide, pecking and probing for worms, shrimps, shellfish and crabs.

Glasswort

Sea sandwort

Eel grass

Feathers

ESTUARY DUMP
The calmer waters of the estuary's tidal inlets are nature's dumping ground for all kinds of seaside debris, from dried-out seaweeds and eel grass to feathers, bits of weeds and dead crabs.

Roots begin to stabilize estuary mud

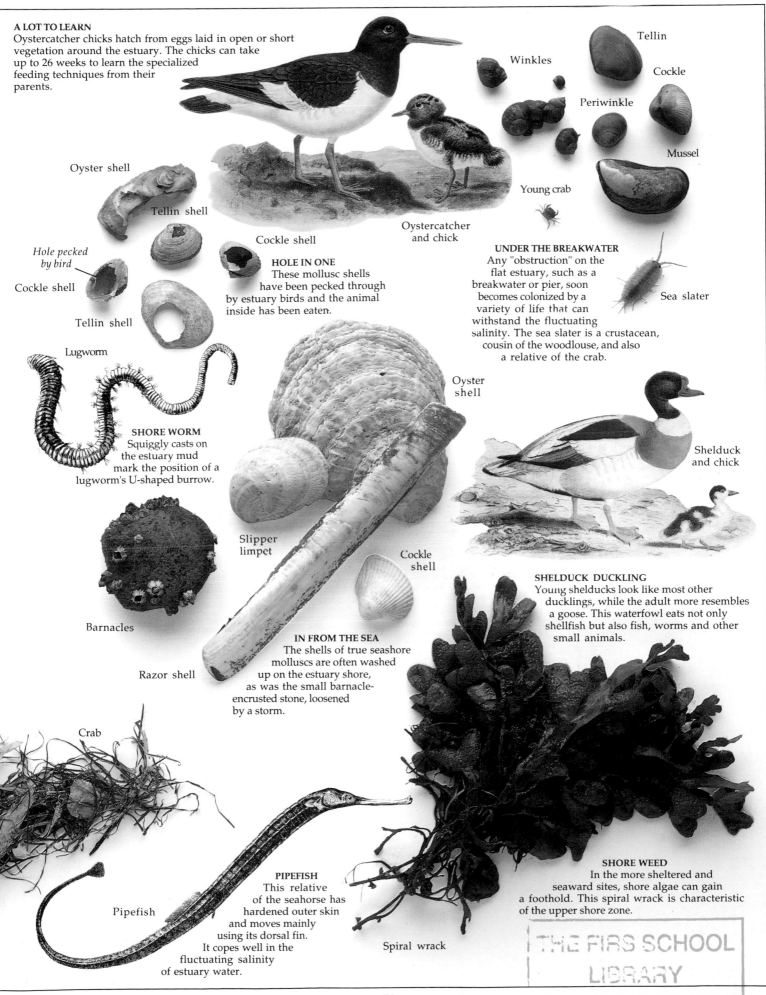

A LOT TO LEARN
Oystercatcher chicks hatch from eggs laid in open or short vegetation around the estuary. The chicks can take up to 26 weeks to learn the specialized feeding techniques from their parents.

Tellin

Winkles

Cockle

Periwinkle

Mussel

Oyster shell

Tellin shell

Cockle shell

Young crab

Oystercatcher and chick

Hole pecked by bird

Cockle shell

Tellin shell

HOLE IN ONE
These mollusc shells have been pecked through by estuary birds and the animal inside has been eaten.

UNDER THE BREAKWATER
Any "obstruction" on the flat estuary, such as a breakwater or pier, soon becomes colonized by a variety of life that can withstand the fluctuating salinity. The sea slater is a crustacean, cousin of the woodlouse, and also a relative of the crab.

Sea slater

Lugworm

SHORE WORM
Squiggly casts on the estuary mud mark the position of a lugworm's U-shaped burrow.

Oyster shell

Shelduck and chick

Barnacles

Slipper limpet

Cockle shell

SHELDUCK DUCKLING
Young shelducks look like most other ducklings, while the adult more resembles a goose. This waterfowl eats not only shellfish but also fish, worms and other small animals.

IN FROM THE SEA
The shells of true seashore molluscs are often washed up on the estuary shore, as was the small barnacle-encrusted stone, loosened by a storm.

Razor shell

Crab

PIPEFISH
This relative of the seahorse has hardened outer skin and moves mainly using its dorsal fin. It copes well in the fluctuating salinity of estuary water.

Pipefish

Spiral wrack

SHORE WEED
In the more sheltered and seaward sites, shore algae can gain a foothold. This spiral wrack is characteristic of the upper shore zone.

59

The salt marsh

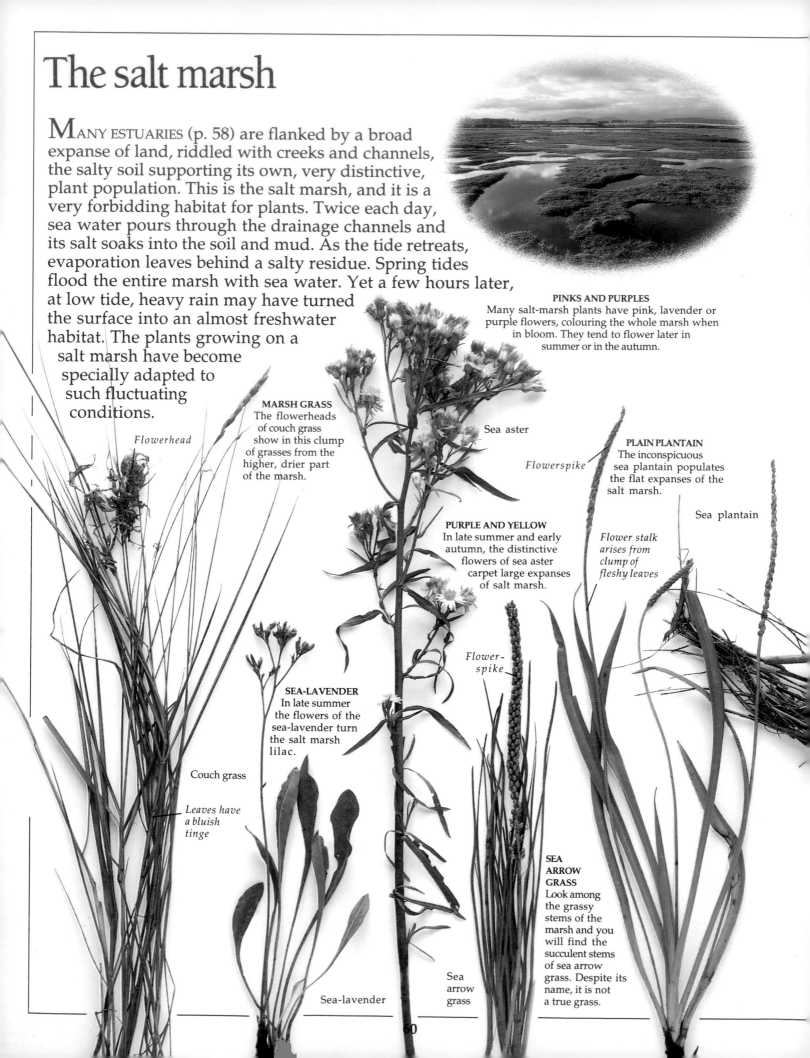

MANY ESTUARIES (p. 58) are flanked by a broad expanse of land, riddled with creeks and channels, the salty soil supporting its own, very distinctive, plant population. This is the salt marsh, and it is a very forbidding habitat for plants. Twice each day, sea water pours through the drainage channels and its salt soaks into the soil and mud. As the tide retreats, evaporation leaves behind a salty residue. Spring tides flood the entire marsh with sea water. Yet a few hours later, at low tide, heavy rain may have turned the surface into an almost freshwater habitat. The plants growing on a salt marsh have become specially adapted to such fluctuating conditions.

PINKS AND PURPLES
Many salt-marsh plants have pink, lavender or purple flowers, colouring the whole marsh when in bloom. They tend to flower later in summer or in the autumn.

Flowerhead

MARSH GRASS
The flowerheads of couch grass show in this clump of grasses from the higher, drier part of the marsh.

Sea aster

PLAIN PLANTAIN
The inconspicuous sea plantain populates the flat expanses of the salt marsh.

Flowerspike

Sea plantain

PURPLE AND YELLOW
In late summer and early autumn, the distinctive flowers of sea aster carpet large expanses of salt marsh.

Flower stalk arises from clump of fleshy leaves

Flower-spike

SEA-LAVENDER
In late summer the flowers of the sea-lavender turn the salt marsh lilac.

Couch grass

Leaves have a bluish tinge

SEA ARROW GRASS
Look among the grassy stems of the marsh and you will find the succulent stems of sea arrow grass. Despite its name, it is not a true grass.

Sea-lavender

Sea arrow grass

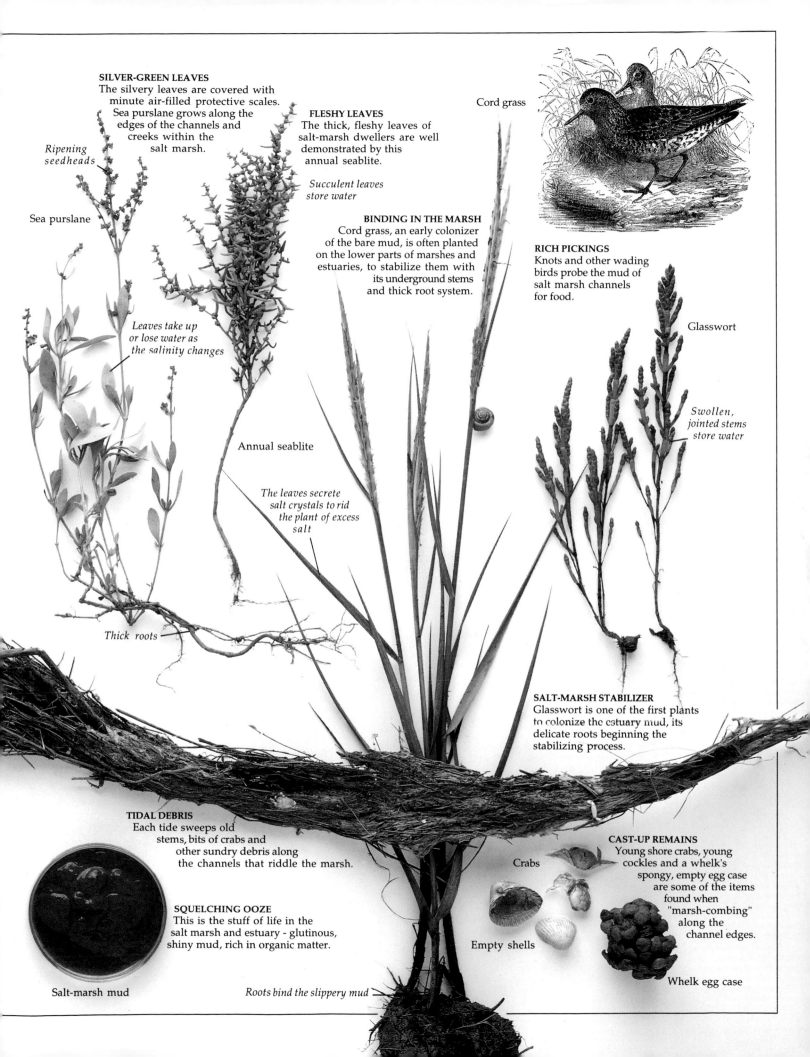

SILVER-GREEN LEAVES
The silvery leaves are covered with minute air-filled protective scales. Sea purslane grows along the edges of the channels and creeks within the salt marsh.

Ripening seedheads

Sea purslane

FLESHY LEAVES
The thick, fleshy leaves of salt-marsh dwellers are well demonstrated by this annual seablite.

Succulent leaves store water

Cord grass

BINDING IN THE MARSH
Cord grass, an early colonizer of the bare mud, is often planted on the lower parts of marshes and estuaries, to stabilize them with its underground stems and thick root system.

RICH PICKINGS
Knots and other wading birds probe the mud of salt marsh channels for food.

Leaves take up or lose water as the salinity changes

Glasswort

Swollen, jointed stems store water

Annual seablite

The leaves secrete salt crystals to rid the plant of excess salt

Thick roots

SALT-MARSH STABILIZER
Glasswort is one of the first plants to colonize the estuary mud, its delicate roots beginning the stabilizing process.

TIDAL DEBRIS
Each tide sweeps old stems, bits of crabs and other sundry debris along the channels that riddle the marsh.

CAST-UP REMAINS
Young shore crabs, young cockles and a whelk's spongy, empty egg case are some of the items found when "marsh-combing" along the channel edges.

Crabs

SQUELCHING OOZE
This is the stuff of life in the salt marsh and estuary - glutinous, shiny mud, rich in organic matter.

Empty shells

Salt-marsh mud

Roots bind the slippery mud

Whelk egg case

Study and conservation

THE FASCINATING WILDLIFE OF PONDS AND RIVERS is suffering in our modern world. Pollution, demand for housing or farming land, and more people using the water for relaxation and recreation are all taking their toll. Conserving and preserving our natural freshwater habitats is increasingly important. It begins with study and understanding. Students of nature are interested in what lives where, and why - and through observation rather than interference. When out on a field trip they have respect for nature, follow the country code, and obey the wildlife laws. If you wish to find out more about ponds and rivers, contact one of the organizations listed on page 64 for guidance on a voyage into nature's watery domain.

THE MICROSCOPIC WORLD
A drop of pond water may look clear, but under a microscope such as this, it will be teeming with tiny water plants and animals. Magnification of about 20X to 200X is most common.

LOOKING THROUGH LENSES
Magnifiers enable you to identify small water creatures or examine a flower's structure. A 10X lens is about right.

Magnifying glasses

Field guide

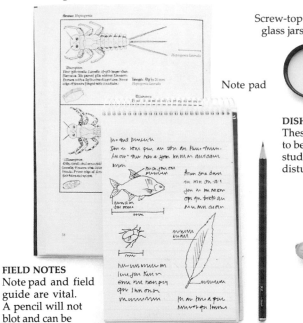

Note pad

Screw-top glass jars

SHORT-STAY HOMES
Screw-top glass jars are useful for temporary storage and examination. Do not leave animals and plants in them for long.

SPOON AND BRUSH
These pieces of equipment enable small, delicate plants and animals to be transferred for study, and then replaced without harm.

DISHES AND DROPPERS
These allow small items to be moved gently and studied without too much disturbance.

FIELD NOTES
Note pad and field guide are vital. A pencil will not blot and can be sharpened carefully with a pocket knife.

Glass dish

Dropper

Plastic spoons

FARM WASTE
Accidental spillage of pig slurry into this river killed chub, dace, roach - and thousands of smaller animals.

Waterproof camera

DAMP-PROOF SNAPS
Modern waterproof cameras allow photographs to be taken in the wettest places, even in the spray of a fast stream. Photos record nature without disturbing it.

The dangers of pollution

Ponds, rivers and other freshwater habitats are under constant threat of pollution. Fertilizers, pesticides and other farming chemicals are washed through the soil by rain and into watercourses, where they may adversely affect the balance of nature. Industrial wastes discharged from factories into rivers can damage water life for long stretches downstream. Most authorities have clean-water laws, but these are not always observed; "accidents" happen, and inspectors cannot monitor every backwater. We can all contribute, by reporting suspicions to the authorities, or by volunteering to help clean out and restock a weed-choked pond, or by clearing a stream used as a rubbish tip.

Fine-mesh sieve

Plastic bags
and ties

Folding
pocket
knife

Secateurs

WATER-PROOFING
Aquatic plants dry out
quickly in air. Keep them
wet during transit in
plastic bags.

A CLEAN CUT
Take plant samples only with permission,
and with a sharp blade for minimum damage.

Trowel

Fork

SIEVE FOR SORTING
A fine-mesh sieve can
be rocked gently in
water to sort small
animals from mud
and silt.

TAKING A SAMPLE
A bucket on a string
can be tossed from a
bridge, bank or boat
to sample the water.

Sealable plastic containers

SPLASH-PROOF CONTAINERS
Pack animals carefully in
sealable containers, using
waterweed as "padding"
to minimize splashing.

SMALL DIGGERS
If you are permitted to dig up plants
or search for muddy-bottom
creatures, use a clean, sharp
fork or trowel and take
great care.

Water-sampling
bucket

Large-mesh net

Fine-mesh net

NET RESULTS
Nets have different mesh
sizes, for large or small specimens.
Exercise caution, so as not to uproot plants.
After sorting, replace the net's contents in the water
as quickly as possible.

Index

A

alder, 19, 20
annual seablites, 61
arrowheads, 14, 20
azolla, 45

B

backswimmers, 51
barnacles, 59
beavers, 37
birch, 19
bithynias, 53
bitterlings, 25
bitterns, 31
bittersweet, 21
blanket weeds, 44
bleak, 22
bream, 23
bullheads, 55

C

caddis flies, 19, 50, 57
carnivores, 10, 12
carp, 12, 13, 24, 25
china mark moths, 43
cockles, 52, 53, 59
common snappers, 41
cord grass, 61
cottongrass, 10
couch grass, 61
crabs, 58, 61

D

damselflies, 48, 49
dippers, 54

dragonflies, 12, 13, 17, 48, 49
drone flies, 50
ducks, 28, 29, 59
duckweeds, 6, 9, 13, 44

E

ecology, 12, 34
eel grass, 47, 58
eels, 22, 24

F

ferns, 54, 55
figwort, 10, 14, 18
flatworms, 13, 20, 57
fool's watercress, 34
freshwater crayfish, 54
freshwater shrimps, 57
frogs, 8, 9, 12, 20, 38,39
fungi, 19, 54

G

glasswort, 58, 61
gnats, 16
grass carp, 25
great burdock, 54
greater spearwort, 15
great woodrush, 54, 55
great willow-herb, 14
grebes, 30, 31
gudgeon, 25
gulls, 58

H

hawthorn, 15
hemp agrimony, 14, 18, 56
herbivores, 10, 12, 17
hermaphrodites, 8
herons, 12, 30, 31

I

Indian balsam, 56
irises, 6, 7, 11, 15, 19, 21, 35, 56, 57

K

kingcups, 7
kingfishers, 30
Kingsley, Charles, 49
knots, 61

L

lady's smock, 6
leeches, 9, 13
lichens, 54
limpets, 53, 59
liverworts, 54
loach, 57
loosestrife, 14
lugworms, 59

M

marestails, 11, 12, 34
marsh marigolds, 7
mayflies, 9, 13, 17, 50-1
meadow rue, 7
meadowsweet, 14
metamorphosis, 12, 48
midges, 16
mink, 12, 36
mosquitoes, 16
mosses, 54, 55
mussels, 52, 53, 59

N

nerites, 52
newts, 8, 9, 12, 16, 19, 38-9
New Zealand pygmyweed, 46

O

oaks, 19, 55
otters, 37, 57
oystercatchers, 58, 59
oysters, 59

P

perch, 23
periwinkles, 59
photosynthesis, 10, 20, 46
pikes, 24
pintail ducks, 18, 29
pipefishes, 59
plankton, 47
pond skaters, 17, 20, 51
poplars, 7
puss moths, 7

R

ragged robin, 10
rat-tailed maggots, 50
razorshells, 59
reed buntings, 30, 31
reed grasses, 6
reedmace, 10, 19, 33, 34, 35
reeds, 6, 10, 21, 32-5
reed warblers, 30, 31
rigid hornwort, 46
roach, 23
rudd, 22
rushes, 14, 18, 32-5, 47

S

St John's-wort, 14-16
salmon, 23
sea arrow grass, 60
sea-aster, 61
sea-lavender, 61
sea plantain, 60
sea purslane, 61
sea spurge, 58
sedges, 6, 11, 18, 19, 32-5
slaters, 9, 12, 59
snails, 8, 12, 16, 19, 20, 52, 53
snakes, 40-41
snipe, 30, 31
spiral wrack, 59
sticklebacks, 9, 17, 25, 51
swans, 18, 28, 29

T

teal, 28
teasels, 56
tellins, 59
tench, 12, 22
toads, 8, 12, 16, 20, 38-9
trout, 26-7
turtles, 41

V

violets, 46, 54
volvox, 46

W

water arum, 10, 14
water beetles, 9, 12, 13, 17, 50-1
water bistort, 14

water boatmen, 13, 16, 51
water crowfoot, 6, 9, 13
water fleas, 8
water forget-me-not, 15
water hawthorn, 17
water hyacinth, 42
water lilies, 8, 10, 20, 34, 42-3, 44
water mites, 13
water plantain, 7, 15, 56, 57
water rail, 31
water shrews, 12, 36
water scorpions, 51
water soldiers, 45
water spiders, 51
water starwort, 47, 57
water stick insects, 17, 51
waterweeds, 19, 47
whelks, 61
widgeon, 28
willows, 7, 11, 15, 19, 21, 34, 35
winkles, 59

Y

yellow flags, 7, 11, 15, 19, 21, 57

Useful addresses

British Naturalist's Association
43 Warnford Road,
Tilehurst, Reading

British Trust for Conservation Volunteers
36 St Mary's Street,
Wallingford, Oxon OX10 0EU

Committee for Environmental Conservation(CoEnCo)
Zoological Gardens, Regent's Park, London NW1 4RY

Field Studies Council
Preston Montford,
Montford Bridge,
Shrewsbury SY4 1HW

Freshwater Biological Society
The Ferry House,
Far Sawrey,Ambleside,
Cumbria LA22 0LP

Royal Society for Nature Conservation
The Green, Nettleham,
Lincoln LN2 2NR

Acknowledgments

Picture credits
t=top b=bottom m=middle l=left r=right

Heather Angel: 43tr; 45br; 53br
G.I. Bernard/Oxford Scientific Films: 51ml
B.Borrell/Frank Lane Picture Agency: 39m
Bridgeman Art Library: 34tr
British Museum/Natural History: 48tl
B.B.Casals/Frank Lane Picture Agency: 39t
John Clegg: 47tl
G.Dore/Bruce Coleman Ltd: 48mr; 60tr
Fotomas Index: 39ml
C.B. and D.W. Frith/Bruce Coleman Ltd: 41br
Tom and Pam Gardener/Frank Lane Picture Agency: 38br
D.T. Grewcock/Frank Lane Picture Agency: 62br

Mark Hamblin/Frank Lane Picture Agency: 39bm
David Hosking/Eric and David Hosking: 27m; 37ml
Mansell Collection: 13m, tr, ml; 35ml; 49br
L.C. Marigo/Bruce Coleman Ltd: 42bl
Mary Evans Picture Library: 22tl; 23tr; 30bl; 40tr
Dr Morley Reed/Science Photo Library: 39bl
Jany Sauvanet/Natural History Photographic Agency: 40ml
Richard Vaughan/Ardea: 58mr
Roger Wilmshurst/Frank Lane Picture Agency: 29t

Illustrations by Coral Mula: 34bl; 36ml, bl, br; 35tl, ml; 38ml, m; 39mt

Picture research by: Millie Trowbridge

Dorling Kindersley would like to thank:
The Booth Museum of Natural History, Brighton.
Ed Wade, and Respectible Reptiles, Hampton, for help with the amphibians and reptiles.
Richard Harrison and Robert Hughes, Upwey Trout Hatchery, for help with the trout eggs.
Jane Parker for the index.
Fred Ford and Mike Pilley of Radius Graphics, and Ray Owen for artwork.
Anne-Marie Bulat for her work on the initial stages of the book.
Carole Ash, Neville Graham and Martyn Foote for design assistance.
Kim Taylor for special photography on page 27.
Dave King for special photography on pages 2-5, 28-31, 36-7, 52-3 and 62-3.

The author would like to thank:
Don Bentley for loan of equipment;
Mike Birch of Mickfield Fish Centre; Max Bond and Tim Watts of Framlingham Fisheries;
CEL Trout Farm, Woodbridge;
Keith Chell and Chris Riley of Slapton Ley Field Centre; Wendy and David Edwards, Ellen and Chris Nall, Jacqui and Tony Storer for allowing their ponds to be sampled; David "Biggles" Gooderham and Jane Parker for help with collecting; Andrea Hanks and staff at Thornham Magna Field Centre; Alastair MacEwan for technical advice;
Ashley Morsely for fish care;
Richard Weaving of Dawlish Warren Nature Reserve;
John Wortley, Andy Wood and colleagues at Anglian Water Authority.